A TOUCH OF SPRING

A comedy

by

SAMUEL TAYLOR

SAMUEL FRENCH

LONDON

NEW YORK TORONTO SYDNEY HOLLYWOOD

CHARACTERS

Presented by John Gale and Allan Davis, in association
with John and Alison Boddington, at the Comedy
Theatre, London, on May 13th, 1975, with the following
cast of characters:

Diana Claiborne	Jill Melford
Alexander Ben Claiborne	Peter Donat
Alison Ames	Hayley Mills
Baldassare Pantaleone	Leigh Lawson
John Wesley	Julian Fellowes
Vittorio Spina	Anthony Morton
Waiter	Ernst Ulman
Assistant Hotel Manager	Bruce Montague
Porter	Lawrence Sewell

The play directed by ALLAN DAVIS
Setting by Carmen Dillon

The action takes place in an apartment in an old hotel,
Rome

ACT I   A day in May

ACT II   A few days later

Time—the present

Please note our NEW ADDRESS:
Samuel French Ltd
52 Fitzroy Street London W1P 6JR
Tel: 01 - 387 9373

ACT I

SCENE 1

An apartment in an old hotel in Rome. A day in May.

The hotel is old, majestic and luxurious, the room is large and light and charming. The walls are of painted panels framed by carved wooden mouldings, painted and gilded, and are their own decoration; there are no pictures or paintings in the room. The ceiling is painted and decorated in the same manner, and has suspended from it a chandelier of Venetian glass. The room has echoes of the eighteenth century: it combines Italian and French rococo and German baroque at their lightest and most graceful. It reminds one vaguely of the Nymphenburg Palace, and the Nymphenburg Blue is here, along with ivory and gold. The colours are gentle and warm

Upstage, in the corners, are two charming cupids in niches, and cupids are very much a part of the painted decoration. The main entrance to the room is up C, double doors raised above the room, opening on to a landing. From the landing, stairs come down to the room from both sides, and framed between these two brief staircases is a marble fountain, another charming cupid. The entrance to the bedroom is down L. High on a wall near it is a small radio speaker; the control knobs are immediately below it. The R wall is taken up by tall glass doors that open on to a planted terrace. Beyond, is Rome. Downstage of the doors is a table on which is the telephone, and an accompanying large upholstered stool. The furniture is a bit shabby, but nice in a warmly romantic way. There is a drinks table or trolley up L, on which are a bottle of Italian aperitif, a bottle of Jack Daniels bourbon, a bottle of San Pellegrino water, an empty ice bucket, and glasses

As hotel rooms go, this one is a great success. It is light and spacious, it is gay, it has a glow

When the CURTAIN rises the sun is pouring in through the open terrace doors. All the bells of Rome are pealing. The radio is playing: we hear an Italian tenor singing "Arrivederci, Roma". The bedroom door opens and Diana Claiborne enters, obviously irritated. Diana is a strikingly handsome American in her early thirties. She is the paradigm of the rich young American married woman: intelligent, witty, aware, sharp, knowledgeable, and hard. She is dressed for travelling, and as she enters she gets rid of her handbag and an over-the-shoulder bag, and crosses angrily towards the terrace. She is followed by her husband, Alexander Ben Claiborne, called Sandy. He is in his thirties, good-looking in a rough sort of way, and he is the quintessence of the successful young American business man: quietly self-assured, with the authority and self-confident good humour that comes with success and position. Sandy is essentially a kind and courteous man, but he has been trained to toughness in the wars of the business world. He is intelligent, he can be witty, and he can also be fiercely impatient. He wears trousers of a lounge suit, and a white shirt open at the neck. He has a narrow bandage wrapped round his left hand. He carries his wife's suitcases, and sets them down in the middle of the room. He looks across at his wife wryly. She stands rigidly angry, staring out at Rome. Then she begins to rap out commands over her shoulder

Diana Turn off that damned radio.

Sandy (*with resigned good humour*) Yep. (*He turns off the radio, and shuts the bedroom door*)

Diana And ring for a porter.

Sandy Yep. (*He moves to the desk to push the buzzer*)

Diana What did you do with my passport?

Sandy Put it in your bag. (*He presses the buzzer*)

Diana (*grimly*) I would like a drink, please.

Sandy (*starting back across to the drinks*) There's no ice.

Diana Whoever heard of an Italian hotel with ice? Just—get me—a drink.

Sandy Yep.

Diana (*glaring out at Rome*) Damn Italy. Damn Rome. Damn all those church bells. (*With true despair, a cry from the heart*) Can't anyone turn off those church bells? (*She turns and slams her bag down on the desk*)

Sandy (*pouring the drink*) Only God or the Pope. Simmer down, Diana.

Diana (*moving towards him; urgently*) Sandy, I want you to fly home with me.

Sandy (*bringing her the drink*) I have got to find my father.

Diana You said it would take two days: we've been here almost a week.

Sandy I didn't know about Italy then. The land of blue skies and red tape. (*Ruefully, as he hands her the drink*) Wouldn't you think when a man dies, someone would remember where they put him?

Diana (*taking the glass*) And what happens in the meantime?

Sandy They're bound to find him sooner or later.

Diana Sandy, they're still looking for the remains of Julius Caesar. (*She takes a belt of the drink and her eyes widen in horror. She stares at it*) What—is—this?

Sandy That Italian drink you said you liked.

Diana (*handing it to him*) Pour it down the sink. It may clear the drains.

Sandy (*moving back to the drinks table*) Do you want some whisky?

Diana (*following him*) No. You could fly home with me and then come back.

Sandy What's so important about me being at your sister's wedding?

Diana (*firmly*) It is important to me.

Sandy And what do I say to my mother! "No, Mother, I have not found Father's body yet, but I shall return to search for him as soon as I've danced with the bride."

Diana (*her eyes narrowing*) Who is more important? Your mother or me?

Sandy That is no question to ask a gentleman. As a matter of fact both of you . . . (*He reconsiders, and starts away to the desk*) Never mind.

Diana Both of us what?

Sandy Nothing. Where the hell is that porter?

Diana (*following him to the desk*) Are you comparing me to your mother?
Sandy (*pressing the buzzer*) Don't hassle me, Diana. I know I've put you through a bad time and I'm sorry, I am sorry.

There is a knock at the door

Ah. Come in.

The door opens and John Wesley appears. He is young and American and scholarly-looking, with horn-rimmed glasses. He is unsure and eager to please. He takes his job seriously and has a tendency to trip over his own feet. He works for the United States Embassy in Rome and carries a brief-case, of course

Wesley Good morning.
Sandy Well, good morning, Mr Wesley, and where the hell have you been?
Wesley (*coming down the L stairs to C*) I tried to call you from the Embassy, but your phone's out of order. Did you know your phone's out of order?
Sandy (*grimly*) Yes, we know our phone's out of order. It is one of the great disasters of the twentieth century. The hotel manager in the striped pants says so, the assistant manager in the striped pants says so. They wring their hands and cry, "Un disastro". What happens in Italy when there really is a disaster?
Diana They wring their hands and lie down.
Wesley That's not fair. The Italians are really very obliging; they're just not very well organized.
Sandy What's so complicated about fixing a phone?
Wesley This isn't America, Mr Claiborne. You've just got to get used to that idea.
Sandy I sure as hell am getting used to it. (*Resigned*) O.K. What's new, what have you got for us? What great defeats have we suffered today?
Wesley (*happily*) Oh no. I've got good news. We have finally and definitely ascertained that your father's body is in Rome.
Diana (*eagerly*) Ah. Where in Rome?
Wesley We don't know.
Sandy Oh, great.
Wesley But that's progress, isn't it? (*With pride*) I knew darned well he wasn't in Naples.
Sandy No. What would he be doing in Naples? Isn't there anyone—anyone at all—who knows where the body is?
Wesley Yes, there is one key official who knows. But no-one can find him.
Diana (*moving to her suitcase with luggage tags*) Maybe he's dead too, sitting next to his phone. (*She sits on the stool next to the armchair and proceeds to put tags on her luggage*)
Wesley (*to Diana*) We'll find him, Mrs Claiborne, don't you worry. Are you going somewhere?
Diana (*with bitter emphasis*) I am going back to America.
Wesley (*horrified*) Without Mr Claiborne's father?
Diana Without Mr Claiborne.

Wesley looks at Sandy questioningly

Sandy (*explaining gently*) My wife's sister is getting married tomorrow, in faraway St Louis, Missouri.
Wesley Can't you postpone it?
Diana Until you find the body? She could be a spinster for the rest of her life.
Sandy Don't be frightened, Mr Wesley. I'm staying.
Wesley Oh.

There is a knock at the door

Waiter Permesso?
Wesley Avanti!

The door opens

Sandy (*looking at Wesley in pain*) Come in.

The Waiter appears. He is a sweet old gentleman

Waiter Signore, you wish for something?
Sandy Me? No.
Diana You rang, remember?
Sandy Oh yes. But I want a porter. (*He moves up to address the Waiter, who remains on the landing*)
Waiter (*in Italian*) Come?
Sandy Porter. I want a porter.
Waiter No, I am not porter. I am waiter.
Sandy But I rang for a porter.
Waiter (*kind but firm*) I am waiter.
Sandy (*hazarding*) How about some coffee?
Waiter Subito, Signore.

The Waiter goes, closing the door

Sandy turns away, rather pleased with himself

Diana How about that? The Great American Tycoon; Harvard Business School; President of The Claiborne-Missouri Tool Company; wants a porter, gets a waiter, settles for coffee.
Sandy (*genially*) In business, that is known as making a deal. Well, Mr Wesley?

Wesley immediately moves to him, fishing a paper out of his briefcase as he goes

Wesley I've brought you that list of top Government officials you asked for. (*He hands Sandy the paper*) The ones marked in red speak English. We think.
Sandy Thank you.
Wesley But frankly, I'm afraid that's not the way to go about it.
Sandy Why not?

Wesley At the Embassy, we have learned that the Italians don't like it if you don't go through channels. (*He puts the briefcase on the table*)

Sandy We've been going through channels for over a week, now. When do we reach the end?

Wesley (*cheerfully*) Well, we just have to keep on trying.

Sandy (*breaking out desperately*) For how long? Mr Wesley! My father died! Suddenly! Tragically! Four thousand miles from home, in a strange country! And I, his son, have come to get him to bring him home. And I *can't get at him*! (*He is deeply moved, close to tears, and turns away quickly to hide his emotion. He stares out of the windows*)

Wesley (*miserably*) I'm terribly sorry.

Sandy (*turning back*) It's O.K.

Wesley notices, for the first time, the bandage on Sandy's hand

Wesley What did you do to your hand?

Sandy (*grimly*) I burned it. In the bathroom. Under the water tap marked "C".

Wesley Oh. You turned on the *Caldo* instead of the *Freddo*. "C" doesn't mean "cold" in Italian. It means "hot".

Sandy I know. I forgot.

Wesley It's really quite simple. "C" for *Caldo*—"Hot". "F" for *Freddo*— "Cold". You've got to remember.

Sandy Or be boiled alive.

Diana As a matter of fact that was the last time we had hot water. (*She rises and picks up her hat from the armchair*)

There is a knock on the door

Waiter (*off*) Permesso?

Wesley Avan . . .

But Sandy stops him with a gesture

Sandy Come in.

Diana goes to tie a tag on her travel bag on the sofa table

The door opens and the Waiter enters with a silver tray on which are tiny cups and saucers, a pot of coffee and a bowl of sugar. He comes down the L stairs to a small coffee table behind the drinks trolley. During the following he puts the tray on the table and puts the table upstage of the stool near the armchair

Diana (*commandingly*) Now, Mr Wesley. Why isn't the American Ambassador doing something about us?

Wesley Oh, he knows about the situation, Mrs Claiborne, and he's very concerned. Honest.

Diana He hasn't returned any of our calls.

Wesley He's very busy.

Diana And very rude. Why can't he see my husband today?

Wesley He had to go north to Florence.

Sandy What for?

Wesley His daughter's competing in a Modern Dance Festival.
Diana Oh, God. (*Defeated, she goes to the mirror on the* R *wall to put on her hat*)
Sandy (*moving to the Waiter*) I hope she does our country proud. Here, let me take that.

The Waiter hands Sandy the bill, and Sandy goes on speaking conversationally as he signs

Do you always use those teeny little cups for coffee?
Waiter Signore?
Sandy (*picking up one of the cups*) This. Don't you ever serve coffee in real cups? I shouldn't have started this. (*He puts down the cup*)
Wesley (*coming to the rescue*) Allow me. (*He approaches the Waiter confidently*) Il signore vorebbe sapere se lei—(*his accent is pretty bad, and his confidence begins to wane*)—forse—qualche volta—puo servire—il caffe nel—una—una . . . (*He can't remember the word for "cup", and desperately grasps for a way out*)—cosa—piu grande!
Waiter (*puzzled*) You mean like for soup?
Sandy (*hastily; returning to the Waiter*) Never mind, forget it, it's O.K., here. (*He hands the Waiter the bill and a tip*)
Waiter Mille grazie, Signore.

The Waiter hurries out

Wesley turns, to find Diana staring at him

Diana (*sweetly*) Mr Wesley, how long have you been in Italy?
Wesley Almost a year.
Diana You have a remarkable gift for languages.

The doors are thrown open and the Assistant Manager appears. He is a cheerful Italian, about forty years old, and he is dressed in a morning coat and striped trousers. Behind him is a Porter. The Waiter passes them, going out. The Porter comes down the L *stairs, gets the luggage and goes out*

Assistant Manager (*as he enters*) Mr Claiborne, Mrs Claiborne, hello! We are ready for you! The car is downstairs!
Diana (*picking up her handbag*) Does it run?
Assistant Manager But of course, it is a Buick! (*To the Porter, as he goes out*) Presto! Presto!

During this, Diana gets her travel bag off the sofa table, pops her handbag into it and goes to Sandy near the stairs L

Diana Well?
Sandy Give my love to the kids.
Diana They may never see their father again. (*She kisses him briefly on the cheek, then turns on Wesley*) I want my husband home for that wedding. I want this finished today, and him on a plane home tonight!
Wesley I'll do my best, Mrs Claiborne.

Diana Don't do your best, make a superhuman effort. Throw your weight around. You're from the United States Embassy. For whatever that means. (*She turns back to the* L *stairs*)

Assistant Manager Everything is going to be all right, Mrs Claiborne.

Diana How old is that Buick?

Assistant Manager Oh, only from nineteen hundred and . . . Not old.

Diana (*to Sandy*) Let's keep in touch, shall we?

Sandy I'll put a note in a bottle.

Diana sails up the stairs

Diana A wonderful invention, the Italian telephone. It ensures total privacy.

Assistant Manager But no, Mrs Claiborne, believe me, there is someone repairing the telephone at this very moment.

Diana (*sweetly*) Leonardo da Vinci, no doubt.

Diana sails out

The Assistant Manager shrugs and starts after her. Sandy turns to the coffee table and sits on the armchair stool next to it, facing downstage

Sandy Coffee?

Wesley (*moving to him*) Yes, please.

As the Assistant Manager starts out, Baldassare Pantaleone slips in through the open doorway, nodding pleasantly to him. The Assistant Manager exits. The doors are closed, leaving Baldassare Pantaleone on the landing looking down at the two men

Baldo (as we shall discover he is called) is a cheerful, laughing Italian in his twenties, quick, darting, smartly dressed. He has dark hair and brilliant, laughing, liquid black eyes. Baldo is an enterprising young Italian, who makes a living being useful to foreigners. He is cunning, intelligent, life-loving, deceitful, affectionate, amoral, cool, shrewd and clever. He is a happy man who has come to terms with life completely. Now, he stands on the landing and watches the men below with a delighted smile. Here is a new adventure

Sandy (*as he pours the coffee*) The thing that gripes me, and it really gripes me, is that we weren't notified of my father's death until two days after the accident.

Wesley Ah, but Mr Claiborne! The accident happened way up in the hills, miles from Rome. By the time the people came from the nearest village, climbed down the mountain to the wreck of the car, gathered up the bodies, brought them back up the mountain . . .

Sandy They've got some kind of communication in Italy, haven't they?

Wesley Oh, when you get up in some of those hill towns, you're back in the nineteenth century.

Sandy We at least had the Pony Express in the nineteenth century.

Baldo lets out a hoot of appreciative laughter, and runs down the R *stairs into the room*

Baldo Ah, that is marvellous! The Pony Express! Cowboys! Indians! Bang,
bang! (*With sudden formality*) Buon giorno. Good morning. You understand, of course, that your telephone is not working.

Sandy It's all yours, pal. Get it done, will you? I've got calls to make.

Baldo (*protesting*) Ma, Signore . . .

Sandy Now, come on! The last guy who was here blew into it twice, put it
down and walked out. You can do better than that.

Baldo Ma, si, but I am not the one who fixes the telephone.

Sandy You're not?

Baldo But if you wish, I will try. (*He goes to the telephone*)

Sandy (*to Wesley*) Isn't there such a thing in Italy as an ordinary, telephone
repair-man?

Baldo picks up the telephone and bangs at the cradle

Baldo Pronto! Pronto! (*He blows into the phone twice, then shrugs and puts
it back in its cradle. He bangs the table hard, then turns back to the
others*) I am sorry, but it is not . . .

The telephone rings

It is working! (*He picks up the phone*) Pronto! Si! E Baldo! Chi e? . . .
Mario! Tu hai reparato il telefono? . . . Ah, bravo! Bravo! . . . Benissimo!
. . . Ah, bravo! . . . Si, bravo! Bravo! Bravo! Bravo! Bravo! Bravo!
(*He hangs up. With a flourish*) That was my cousin. He fixed the tele-
phone. (*He goes smoothly to Sandy*) Mr Claiborne, you must know
that I did not come here because the telephone was not working. No.
I came because the telephone was not working and so I could not tell
you I was coming, and so I came. My name is Baldassare Pantaleone.

Wesley Oh!

Baldo You know me.

Wesley The Embassy uses him, sometimes, for special problems . . .

Baldo Si! I have come to help you, Mr Claiborne. Mr Alexander Ben
Claiborne, from San' Louee, Missouri. (*He refers to a small notebook
which he takes out of his pocket*)

Sandy (*mechanically*) Saint Louis.

Baldo Va bene. San' Louee. (*With sad, liquid eyes*) I am sorry for you, Mr
Claiborne, in this tremendous disastro, the loss of your beloved father,
Joseph Claiborne. I will tell you truly, all of my country mourns for
him, this good friend of the Italian people, this great and famous
American . . .

Sandy You knew him.

Baldo No. This lady I have seen go out: this is your wife?

Sandy Yes.

Baldo Very good-looking. She could not stay?

Sandy No.

Baldo You Americans are always in a hurry. Ah, but now! I am here to
help you: you wish to take your father back to America for the funeral:
it is for this the Ambassador has sent me.

Sandy The American Ambassador?

Baldo Certo. We are old friends. He calls me many times, when the visiting Americans are getting in his hair . . .

Wesley (*quickly*) Mr Pantaleone . . .

Baldo But not you. No. No. No. The Ambassador has called me yesterday and he has said: "Baldo, I have this good friend, Mr Alexander Ben Claiborne from San' Louee, Missouri . . ."

Sandy (*mechanically*) St Louis.

Baldo Va bene, San' Louee, "a rich and famous American of great position and high birth, who makes tools. And he has suffered this sad disastro and I would like to help him, but I must go to Florence . . ."

Sandy (*impassively*) What do you charge?

Baldo Pardon?

Sandy What do you charge?

Baldo (*forgiving him*) I have come to help you . . .

Sandy (*inexorably*) What do you charge?

Baldo (*tightening*) I do this for you in your distress because I love America and all Americans . . .

Sandy (*to Wesley*) Does the Ambassador pay for this, or do I?

Baldo (*with a small, polite bow*) Buon giorno. (*He turns and starts to walk out*)

Sandy (*rising*) Wait a minute!

Baldo (*immediately and joyfully returning to him*) No, you are right, we must not quarrel, we are friends! (*He shakes Sandy's hand vigorously*) We will not speak of money . . .

At this moment the telephone rings, and Baldo immediately starts for it quickly

Sandy Wait a minute!

Baldo stops

I'll get it. (*He crosses past Baldo and picks up the phone*) Hello! . . . Hello! . . . Hello! (*He is getting no answer*) God damn it!

Baldo glides swiftly to Sandy's side and stamps hard on the floor, making Sandy jump a little in surprise)

Hello! . . . Yes, this is Mr Claiborne.

Sandy glances at Baldo, who shrugs modestly

Yes, I know: It's been out of order since yesterday. Who is this? . . . I beg your pardon? . . . Am I supposed to know you? . . . Alison Ames? (*He looks over at Wesley*)

Wesley shakes his head

Well, is it about my father's death? . . . Oh! Well, where are you? . . . Yes! Please! Come right up! (*He hangs up*) Alison Ames.

Wesley No, never heard of her. Here. I forgot. I'm sorry. (*He takes a paper from his briefcase*)

Sandy What is it?

Wesley Another form for you to sign. (*He moves to Sandy, so that Baldo is between them*)

Sandy That's all I do.

Wesley Oh, they've got a million of 'em.

Baldo (*taking the outstretched paper*) Prego. Allow me. (*He scans it*) Ho, si. It is very necessary. (*Reading*) "*Responsibilita della Republica Ital . . .*" si. (*Moving below the desk*) You can do nothing without this. It is the guarantee.

Sandy Of what?

Baldo That you will not sue the Italian Government.

Sandy For what?

Baldo Oh, say you find your father, and he does not look so good . . .

Sandy Tear it up! God damn it! (*He tries to take the paper*)

Baldo (*resisting*) No, no, you must sign it. Sign everything. It is the only way. Please. You will sign, yes? Please? (*He leans towards Sandy across the desk, offering the paper and a pen, and smiles at him with warm pleading charm. His smile is almost coquettish*)

After a moment, Sandy reluctantly takes the pen and signs the paper. Baldo retrieves the pen and paper, folds the paper and puts it in his pocket with a grand flourish

Good. Done. From now on, you have no worry: Baldo is here.

There is a knock at the door

Avanti!

Wesley Avanti!

Sandy Come in!

The door opens, and Alison Ames appears on the landing. She is a young Englishwoman, slim, straight and fair. The first impact of this girl is to suggest a unique directness in the way she looks at the world. There is sophistication here in the true sense, coupled with straightforwardness and an almost painful lack of guile. Alison is an actress, and a not very successful one, perhaps because she has too much humour and too much of a sense of the ridiculous to be able to take herself seriously. This is a girl of honest appetites and a felicity for living. But at this moment she is serious and self-contained, giving the sense of troubled anxiety deep within, and a feeling of loss. She looks down at the men

Alison Mr Claiborne?

Sandy (*moving to the foot of the L stairs*) Miss Ames? Please come down.

Alison comes down, and Sandy leads her into the room as he introduces the others

This is John Wesley of the American Embassy . . .

Alison and Wesley shake hands. Wesley moves down L

And Mr . . .

Baldo (*coming to Alison*) Pantaleone. Baldassare Pantaleone. (*He kisses her hand, and backs away*)

Alison turns to Sandy and smiles gravely

Alison I'm sorry about your father.

Sandy You said you had something to tell me.

Alison No, I came in the hope that you might have something to tell me.

Sandy About what?

Alison My mother. The British Embassy is no help at all. They seem quite bewildered at finding themselves in a foreign country. (*She smiles at Wesley*) You're not like that, are you? (*To Sandy*) But at least they did know your father's name, and called the American Embassy and found out you were here. And so I came to see you.

Sandy Why?

Alison To see if we should join forces, so to speak. I can *not* get permission to see my mother. I really do think . . . (*To Baldo—her sense of helplessness is beginning to show*) I thought Italians were supposed to be so obliging!

Baldo makes a gesture as she turns back to Sandy

It isn't that I want to see her, really. I'd much rather remember her as she was. But I do want to know that she's there! (*And she is suddenly close to tears. She sits down on the sofa, and catches hold of herself*) Damn. I'm sorry. But it's all been so sudden and strange. To find yourself whisking off to another country to . . . (*She almost visibly shakes away her distress, and makes an attempt at a smile*) I am sorry. Have you been able to see your father?

Sandy (*wondering*) No, I haven't.

Alison It is maddening, isn't it? One can't even find out where they are.

Sandy "They?"

Alison My mother and your father.

Sandy What have they to do with each other?

Alison Why, they're together, I believe. Side by side, I expect.

Baldo (*understanding the situation*) Madonna mia! (*And, wringing his hands, he moves away from them towards the windows*)

Alison Does he know where they are? Mr . . .?

Baldo (*with a gesture of innocence*) No, no—I do not know.

Alison Do you think it's the public mortuary, or the morgue, or whatever they call it, here?

Sandy Why?

Alison What?

Sandy Why are they together? Side by side? Your mother and my father?

Alison (*staring at him*) Wasn't your father killed in a car accident?

Sandy Yes.

Alison My mother was killed in the same accident.

Sandy You mean they ran into each other?

Alison That would have been difficult, since they were in the same car.

Wesley Oh, my!

Sandy Your mother was in my father's car?

Alison Yes.

Sandy What was she doing there?

Alison Travelling.

Sandy With my father?
Alison Yes.
Sandy Why?
Alison Why do you think people travel together? For company.
Sandy But how did she . . . (*He whirls on Wesley*) What is this?
Wesley I don't know!
Sandy You told me it was an Italian hitch-hiker!
Alison (*rising*) A what?
Wesley That's what we thought.
Sandy Thought!
Wesley Well, the police told us that the person riding with your father was
  not an American . . .
Alison (*sharply*) Of course not, she was English!
Sandy (*driving*) And you didn't bother to check?
Wesley We don't automatically. We're only concerned with Americans.
Sandy (*appalled*) Only concerned with . . .
Alison Ah, no, he's quite right. Do not ask for whom the bell tolls, if it
  doesn't toll for an American.
Wesley I'm terribly sorry.
Sandy (*in cold anger*) And I would be terribly obliged if you would look
  into this matter. And find out exactly what happened. (*He moves swiftly
  round the room gathering Wesley's hat and briefcase*) And when. And
  how. And why my father was responsible for the death of Miss Ames's
  mother.
Alison (*quickly*) But he wasn't!

*Sandy dumps the hat and briefcase into Wesley's arms, and Wesley starts up
the stairs, chagrined and embarrassed*

Wesley Yes, of course, I'll go right back to the Embassy . . .
Sandy (*at the foot of the stairs, with fierce command*) And let me know at
  once!

*And with that, Wesley takes his hand off the doorknob, turns on Sandy
bravely, and speaks from the landing, his voice trembling a little*

Wesley Mr Claiborne, I know you're an important businessman, but I
  don't think you understand exactly what an American Embassy is
  supposed to do.
Sandy I don't give a damn what you're supposed to . . .
Wesley I do! (*He gathers himself, and pours it out with all the dignity he
  can muster*) The role of the American Embassy abroad is to support
  United States foreign policy. That is all! Anything we do for Americans
  coming through here is a politeness, a courtesy, and not an obligation.
  Do you know what I'm called on to do for my fellow Americans? (*He is
  now addressing them all, and God*) I find shirt-makers! And foot doctors!
  And baby-sitters! And opera tickets! I send flowers, I send packages, I
  find umbrellas, I take care of dogs! And for this I went to the Graduate
  School of International Studies at Washington. I'm expected to find
  hotel accommodations when there aren't any to be found. I found
  yours, and you don't like them . . .

Sandy (*moving away with a wave that takes in the room*) All I wanted was a room and bath, not this bower of cupids!

Wesley It's all I could get! And it isn't exactly a hovel! (*By now he is pretty emotional and close to tears*) I'm sorry about your father. I'm sorry we're having such difficulties. I'm sorry about this mix-up, I think it's awful. But I didn't invent two thousand years of Italian red tape, I'm just a second assistant secretary! And if you want to report me to your Congressman when you get home, *please feel free!* (*And, holding back the tears, he turns quickly to go out*)

Sandy (*whipping back to the foot of the stairs*) Mr Wesley! I apologize!

At the same time, Wesley whips around to him desperately

Wesley (*simultaneously*) Mr Claiborne, I apologize! I shouldn't have said that. You've been very patient.

Sandy Not at all, I've been a son-of-a-bitch.

Wesley Oh, no! When you consider what you've been through . . .

Sandy No, I've been a real bastard, forgive me.

Wesley But I should have done better . . .

Sandy You did all that you could.

Wesley No, really, I'm sorry . . .

Wesley takes one step down, Sandy takes one step up, and they shake hands vigorously

Sandy I'm the one to be sorry.

Wesley Not at all.

Sandy Yes, I am.

Wesley Not at all.

Sandy Not at all.

They are still shaking hands

Wesley Miss Ames , . .

Alison Oh, please don't stop. I've never seen two Americans make love before.

Sandy looks down at her, surprised and amused

Wesley (*sincerely*) Miss Ames, I don't know how to apologize for this. But if there's anything I can do, any way I can make up for it, I'd be grateful if you'd call me and . . . (*Then, hopelessly*) Ah, hell, I probably couldn't do anything anyway.

Wesley turns and goes out

They look after him. Baldo comes alive

Baldo Mr Wesley, wait! (*He runs up the* R *stairs*) I must find out who he has talked to, where he has been, who in the Government . . . (*To Sandy and Alison, hastily*) Stay! Wait! Don't go away! (*He dashes out of the door, calling*) Mr Wesley! I have a cousin who is obliging the foreign minister!

And Baldo is gone

Sandy comes down the stairs to Alison

Sandy I'm sorry. I must have seemed terribly rude.

Alison I'd no idea you didn't know about my mother.

Sandy No, I didn't. I do apologize.

Alison (*echoing Wesley*) Not at all. I apologize! (*And she puts out her hand*)

Sandy (*laughing*) Not at all. (*He shakes her hand*) I shouldn't have blown my stack like that.

Alison It was understandable. (*Admiring the room*) He did well by you, you know. The British Embassy, with majestic grace and favour, actually found me a hovel.

Sandy (*moving the coffee table out of the way*) It is quite a room, isn't it? This is the Royal Suite.

Alison (*gazing about, wandering*) Can you afford it?

Sandy Yes.

Alison Of course. It's super.

Sandy It used to be an Italian palazzo. You should see the bedroom.

Alison Big?

Sandy Enormous. I kept losing my wife.

Alison Your wife?

Sandy She went back to America this morning.

Alison Ah. (*Still wandering*) How marvellous—I've an affection for seedy grandeur.

Sandy I suppose that's because you're English. (*And then he curses himself*) I'm terribly sorry.

Alison Not at all, you're right. Seedy grandeur *is* the affliction, isn't it?

Sandy I suppose I am lucky to have this. It was being held for the Prime Minister of some African country, but they cancelled at the last minute.

Alison Oh? Did somebody shoot him?

Sandy (*with a delighted yelp*) Yes! Really!

Alison Well, it's an ill wind . . . (*She turns to the terrace*) What a heavenly view!

Sandy (*behind her, pointing*) Those are the Pines of Rome.

Alison I didn't know they had special pines. I'm awfully ignorant. (*She notices the bandage*) What happened to your hand?

Sandy I turned on the *Caldo* instead of the *Freddo*.

Alison (*grinning*) So did I. And made a flying leap out of the bath. It was quite a sight.

Sandy I'll bet.

They smile companionably. She turns down to the sofa

(*Looking serious*) Miss Ames, I can't tell you . . .

Alison (*turning*) Ah, you're about to apologize again. Please don't. Your father didn't kill my mother.

Sandy In a way.

Alison What nonsense. They were travelling together.

Sandy And he was driving.

Alison And they had an accident, that's all. Unless you think he was making a pass at her at the moment, and took his eyes off the road and his hands off the wheel. Do you suppose that's how it happened?

Sandy My father wasn't the kind of man who makes passes at strange women.

Alison (*coldly*) My mother was not a strange woman. (*She sits on the sofa*)

Sandy No, obviously they'd met. How did they meet? Do you know? (*He sits on the desk stool, facing her*)

She measures him speculatively

Alison My mother and your father.

Sandy Mmm.

Alison You don't know.

Sandy No. Do you?

Alison (*at the moment of decision*) No.

Sandy Well, I suppose they met the way tourists usually do . . .

Alison Most likely.

Sandy They were probably staying at the same hotel in Florence or Venice . . .

Alison Perugia.

He looks at her. She smiles brightly

Florence and Venice have been done so much, don't you think?

Sandy (*conceding*) Ah, well—yes—Perugia—and they probably happened to speak to each other in the lobby . . .

Alison (*helping along*) Probably at the desk, getting their mail . . .

Sandy Yes! The sort of thing people do. Don't you think so?

Alison Or a shop? What about a shop?

Sandy (*considering*) Yes . . .

Alison A shop sounds more fun.

Sandy (*getting into the spirit of it*) Yes, all those tourists. And your mother might have been trying to buy something from a salesman who didn't speak English, and my father came to her rescue . . .

Alison Lovely idea. Make a good film.

Sandy Yes!

Alison Cary Grant and my mother.

Sandy (*enjoying it*) I don't think Cary Grant speaks Italian.

Alison I don't think it would matter.

Sandy (*laughing*) And my father's Italian was very good. He came to Italy every year.

Alison Alone?

Sandy (*very much at ease now*) Yes. His yearly sabbatical, from the family and the job. He loved to wander about Italy alone, for a month every year.

Alison Sounds lovely. And then what?

Sandy (*working it out logically*) Well—my father had a car—and I guess he was on his way to Rome——

Alison —and he discovered that my mother was going to Rome——

Sandy —and so he offered her a lift——

Alison —for which she was eternally grateful.

Sandy (*rising, startled*) Well . . .

Alison And they lived happily ever after for several hours, and then went over the side of a mountain, and were killed.

Sandy (*crossing the room*) What a damned-fool senseless thing. And so cruelly ironic that your mother, a stranger . . .

Alison (*firmly*) Please stop calling her a stranger.

Sandy (*startled*) Oh! I'm sorry!

Alison (*with a touch of hardness*) I wonder what they said to each other as they went over the edge?

He stares at her

Do you never think of things like that? I've often wished I could collect the last words of people as they go hurtling to their death. Or do you suppose they say something terrible prosaic, like "Damn!"?

Sandy I've said something to annoy you.

Alison No, really not. I think you've worked out a very acceptable story.

Sandy It makes sense, doesn't it?

Alison Oh, very good sense.

Sandy I just hope I don't have to use it, that's all.

Alison What do you mean?

Sandy (*wandering down* L) I've got a problem. How do I go about explaining to my mother that my father was found dead with a . . . another woman?

Alison Do you have to make it sound so—improper?

Sandy (*with a small smile*) No matter how it's told to my mother, it will sound improper.

Alison Ah. Of the old school, is she?

Sandy Yes.

Alison (*rising and moving to him as she speaks*) I suspect you come of an intensely respectable American family. Do you?

Sandy Yes.

Alison Heartland of America, and all that?

He nods

Puritan stock? Oh pioneers?

Sandy Yes.

Alison considers him with grave amusement for a moment

Alison Don't tell her. Tell her it was that Italian hitch-hiker. Mr Wesley and the American Embassy will swear to it.

Sandy laughs, liking her very much

Sandy Would you like a drink?

Alison I'd love one.

Sandy (*going to the drinks table*) Something Italian, or bourbon, from the Heartland of America?

Alison Oh, Heartland of America, of course!

Baldo opens the door and puts his head in

Baldo Permesso!

Alison (*blithely*) Avanti!

Baldo (*entering cheerfully*) Ho! You speak very good Italian!

Alison I know three words: "Avanti"! and "Non Disturbare" from the sign on my hotel room door, which, I assume, means "Do Not Disturb".

Baldo Very good!

Sandy And with those three words, a girl can go far. (*Pouring whiskies and water*) No ice.

Baldo (*happily*) American whisky? I love American whisky!

Sandy You shall have some. Now, will you please explain this "Permesso-Avanti!" thing. Do you have to say it all the time?

Baldo It is like your "Is anyone in?", or "Can I come in?", but more simple. And more polite, yes? Here, if someone wishes to enter, he asks, "Permesso?" And if you wish him to enter, you say, "Avanti!" Forward!

Sandy Suppose you don't wish him to enter?

Alison (*triumphantly*) Non Disturbare!

Baldo Brava!

Sandy (*handing a glass to Alison*) American whisky.

Alison Thank you. (*She sits in the armchair L*)

Baldo (*to Sandy*) What have you done to your hand? No, don't tell me. I can guess. *Caldo-freddo*, yes? Hah! You all do it!

Sandy (*handing him a drink*) I know, we lose more Americans, that way.

Baldo (*raising his glass*) Welcome to Rome! (*He drinks and sighs euphorically*) Ahhhhh!

Sandy (*moving to the sofa with his whisky and sitting R*) I'd been given to understand you Italians never drink hard liquor.

Baldo (*standing between them*) It only seems like never. Do you know how much a bottle of your Mr Jack Daniels costs on the Via Veneto? (*To Alison*) You are beautiful.

Alison (*amused*) Thank you. Are you with the government?

Baldo Me? I am against the government! (*He makes a rude noise*) I work for you! For him! For you for love, for him for money. (*He grins at Sandy*) Also love. D'accordo? Agreed?

Sandy Mr Pantaleone is going to conduct us through the labyrinths of Italian bureaucracy. I have just hired him, for God knows how much.

Baldo Almost nothing. And worth every dollar. You will see. Ah, we are going to be so happy together, we three!

Sandy Happy!

Baldo (*hastily*) No, no, I know! Sad! It is terrible! Your father, your mother! Un disastro! I am sorry for you to beat the band!

Alison (*drily*) But one can't be sorry for twenty-four hours of the day, can one?

Baldo You have it! One carries the tears in the pocket. There is a time to sorrow, a time to mourn, but one also must eat, must drink, one sleeps——

Alison —life goes on!

Baldo Appunto! Ah, you are a brave girl to come to Rome alone, this way, to find your dead mother. Your father was desolated and could not come, eh?

Alison I'm afraid my father's dead, too.

Baldo looks stricken

Oh, it wasn't anything recent. He died shortly after the war.

Baldo How terrible. What war?

Alison (*staring at him*) Didn't you have a war?

Baldo Oh, you mean Mussolini. That. (*He shrugs*) That was a mistake. (*He examines Alison caressingly*) Alison Ames. Alison Ames. When I have seen you come into the room, Alison Ames. Che belleza! You are a dream of fair English woman. The way you walk; the look; the legs so straight; the shine of the hair; the eyes like moonlight; the breasts not big and round like the Italians, but small and high and lovely and pointed. Che bella ragazza! (*He turns on Sandy*) And you!

Sandy quickly crosses his arms over his chest

Alexander Ben Claiborne! When I have come into the room and seen you! So American handsome! Such power and strength! (*He swaggers over to Sandy*) How you move across the room like a—like a—that animal you have in the West . . .

Sandy A high-breasted buffalo. Look, Mr Pantaleone . . .

Baldo Baldo. You will call me Baldo. My name is Baldassare, si, I am one of the three wise men who brought gifts to the little Jesus . . .

Alison Oh! (*She sings*) "We Three Kings of Orient Are . . ."

Baldo Ecco! Caspar! Melchior! Baldassare! You will teach me that song, please?

Alison (*nodding happily*) Yes. But I'd much rather call you Baldassare. Such a lovely name.

Baldo No, Baldo. All of Rome calls me Baldo. You will see. When we walk down the Via Veneto, people at the sidewalk cafes will call, "Baldo!" When we go to the Piazza del Popolo, people will stand up across the piazza and shout—(*and he waves and shouts*)—"BAL——DO!!!!!!!"

Alison It doesn't make for much of a private life, does it? Exactly what is it you do, Mr Pantaleone?

Baldo Baldo.

Alison Baldo. Besides finding dead people?

Baldo I am an Assistant.

Sandy Assistant what?

Baldo Whatever you wish.

Alison To whom?

Baldo Whoever wishes. You, him, anyone who needs assistance, in Rome, in Italy, wherever. It is for this I am famous. I speak all languages. People, when they come to Rome, they call Baldo. Business men, diplomats, film companies, big stars from Hollywood, I know them all, I am always The Assistant. I know everybody, I oblige everybody, I am useful to everybody, I am The Professional Assistant.

Sandy (*suspecting*) How far does this go?

Baldo As far as you like.

Sandy Night work, too?

Baldo Certo. One cannot do business twenty-four hours a day.

Sandy (*with a glint of a grin*) And so, if a client wants to relax a little at night . . .

Baldo I am The Assistant.

Alison You mean you get girls for men?

Baldo (*shrugging*) Girls for men, men for girls, girls for girls, men for men.

Sandy That just about covers everything but sheep, doesn't it?

Baldo (*genially*) Oh, sheep, too. (*He sits on the edge of the sofa and grins fondly at Sandy*)

Alison What you'd call a mixed bag.

Sandy As a paid assistant, are you ever asked to—assist in bed?

Baldo (*cheerfully*) Many times. But for this I do not ask to be paid.

Sandy You throw that in.

Baldo I like to keep my clients happy.

Sandy (*to Alison*) How about that?

Alison An interesting line of work.

Baldo You do not know the half. (*To Sandy*) I can see you do not approve.

Sandy (*bravely, reassuring*) Who, me? No, no, it's all right. (*He rises to take the empty glasses and return them to the drinks table*) I've been around—I've been arrested for speeding . . .

Baldo It is all for fun. (*He rises and moves part of the way towards Sandy*) In Rome, vice is not a problem, it is part of living. And I assure you, most of my clients are Anglo-Saxon.

Sandy I believe it. No, fine! Good luck! (*He moves back towards Baldo*)

Alison Well, he does fill a need, doesn't he?

Sandy Yes, I don't think the computer's going to put *him* out of business.

Baldo laughs with delight at the remark, and takes advantage of it to pull Sandy around to him, slap his cheeks affectionately, throw his arms around him and hug him

Baldo Oh, that is marvellous! You have said it! I will tell it to all of Rome! The computer will not take Baldo's place, mai! Never! (*He is wrapped around Sandy and is biting his ears*)

Sandy tries to free himself. Alison watches with interest

Sandy All right. All right. All right! (*He breaks loose*) Stop horsing around! We've got business to attend to.

Baldo immediately becomes brisk and businesslike. He is no fool

Baldo Si. Yes. Business. We must attend to business.

Sandy (*going to the desk*) O.K. Let's get organized. The first step is to find the bodies, right? My father, Miss Ames's mother.

Baldo (*all business*) Right. (*He gets out his little notebook and makes notes*)

Sandy Then, having found them—you can find them——

Baldo You can believe it.

Sandy —the next step will be to get permission to ship them out of the country. Is that right?

Baldo Absolutely right.

Sandy And you can do that. You know where to go, who to see, what

forms to fill out, who has to sign them, how to get them signed, everything. Right?

Baldo Absolutely!

Sandy O.K. Let's get started. (*He gathers up some papers*)

Baldo O.K. We go to lunch. (*He closes his notebook and speeds towards the stairs*)

Sandy closes his eyes in pain

Sandy (*rising*) Wait a minute!

Baldo (*speeding up the stairs to the landing*) It is a quarter past one, there
is a restaurant in the Piazza del Popolo that saves a table always for me.
And we will have such a lunch.

Alison (*going to get her bag*) Sounds super. I'm famished.

Sandy I want to see some people first.

Baldo There is no-one to see. Everything is closed until four o'clock.

Sandy Four o'clock! What do they do until four o'clock?

Baldo They eat, they sleep, they . . . Time passes.

Sandy Let's phone somebody!

Baldo No-one will answer.

Sandy The world doesn't come to a stop between one and four!

Alison It seems it does. Ah, come along. When in Rome, you know . . .

Sandy (*sternly*) No, I don't know. Why do you have to do as the Romans
do, when you can do things better and faster?

Alison (*gently*) Do you have to do things better and faster?

Sandy Yes, ma'am.

Alison Why?

Sandy Why do you have to breathe?

*Alison is interested in this man, and would like to probe further, but Baldo
takes over*

Baldo (*on the landing; firmly*) No! He is right! Absolutely! It is The
American Way! This is The American Century! (*To Sandy*) Once we
were like you. Yes. The Romans. We knew how to do things. We were
the leaders of the Western World. We brought our civilization to the
backward countries. We conquered the world, we ruled the world! The
Pax Romana! (*Nicely*) But then we gave it up, it was too much trouble.

*Alison laughs, and Sandy has to grin his appreciation. Baldo smiles winningly,
and runs down the stairs to Sandy*

And ever since then we have been very happy. You do not mind my
saying this . . .

Alison Ah, do come along, it's just a few hours. One does have to wait for
things in this world, doesn't one? It usually works out in the end.

Sandy (*hopelessly*) That's the most English thing I've ever heard.

Alison But then I am English. And he's Italian. And we're playing the
game by his rules, not ours. Come along.

Sandy gives up, and starts for the bedroom

Sandy I just wish I knew what the rules are.

Baldo It is difficult to explain.

Alison Maybe the basic rule is that there are no rules.

Sandy (*at the door*) I'd bet the other way. They've probably got so many rules, that breaking them is the national pastime.

Sandy goes into the bedroom, closing the door

Alison goes to the mirror on the wall R *to arrange her hair, etc.*

Baldo Ecco. He is smart. When you are young, in Italy, you are taught all the good rules. That is beautiful. When you are a little older, you learn that if you try to live by these beautiful rules, you will end up with no hands and no feet. That is life. (*He lolls on the sofa, watching her*)

Alison And so you break them.

Baldo We—go under them—over them—around them . . . Are you married?

Alison No.

Baldo You have been married?

Alison No.

Baldo Are you a virgin?

A smiling no-answer

No. You have a lover?

Alison Not at the moment.

Baldo You will like an Italian lover.

Alison (*moving to him; grinning*) I don't expect to stay long enough to find one. But I may come back. Shall I write ahead and describe to you what I'd like? Height, weight, colour of eyes, favourite flower, state of mind?

Baldo You will have no trouble. Besides, I will offer myself, first.

Alison You are kind. But I suspect you're more interested in him than in me. (*She nods to the bedroom*)

Baldo (*grinning*) I am a man of catholic tastes.

Alison You won't mind too much if I rule myself out.

Baldo It would be a pity. There are things I could show you in Rome . . .

Alison (*with a wicked smile*) Thank you—no.

Baldo (*studying her*) I have seen you before.

Alison Oh, that's unworthy of you. (*She moves past him to the centre of the room*)

Baldo No, truly. Since you first came into the room.

Alison I shouldn't think so. Unless you also have a taste for British television commercials, and that would be a bit bizarre, even for you.

Baldo (*happily enlightened*) Ah! You are an actress!

Sandy enters, closing the door on the last word. He has put on a coat and tie

Alison (*to both of them; firmly*) Yes. Yes, I am.

Baldo Then I have seen you.

Alison I doubt it. Have you ever seen a British television commercial?

Baldo I think so.

Alison This one? (*She puts down her bag and kicks off her shoes*)

Sandy sits in the armchair L to watch, Baldo is on the sofa. Alison plunges into the commercial, playing all the parts, acting it out with swift skill. It goes something like this. First: as the mother

Daphne, darling! Come to Mummy, darling! (*As the little girl*) No, you muthn't touch me! You've got rough hands! (*As the mother*) Rough hands! Oh, what shall I do? (*As a sound effect*) Phoom! (*As the mother*) Oh! Who are you? (*As the pixie*) I am your Pixie Godmother. (*As a sound effect*) Tinkle, tinkle, tinkle. (*As the pixie*) And I have brought you the gift of velvet hands. (*As the mother*) Thank you! (*She takes the imaginary package. As a sound effect*) Phoom! (*As the mother*) Oh! (*She squeezes the imaginary bottle*) Squish, squish, dip, dip. (*She dips her hands in the imaginary suds, then takes them out to admire them*) Velvet hands! Velvet hands! Daphne, darling, come to Mummy, darling! (*As the little girl*) Oh, Mummy, your hands are tho thoft! (*As the mother*) That's because Pixie Liquid has come into my life. (*As the little girl*) It doesn't make the plates thoft. (*As the mother*) No, my darling. (*As the little girl*) Thoft plates would be thilly. (*As the mother*) Yes, my darling. Would you like to be Mummy's little helper? Come along. (*As a sound effect*) Phoom! (*As the pixie, she strikes a ballet pose, and dances gracefully across the stage to Baldo, singing*) "Hands that wash up can be soft as your face/With wonderful Pixie Liquid." (*She drops a deep curtsy before Baldo, and smiles up at him*)

Baldo (*stunned*) This I have not seen.

Alison rises and smiles at Sandy, not a bit self-conscious

Sandy (*rather impressed*) Very good.

Baldo (*rising*) But I have seen you in films.

Alison (*sitting on the sofa and putting on her shoes*) I doubt that, too. I've been in three, but if you blinked, you missed me.

Sandy (*moving to her*) Is that how you make your living? (*He makes a quick gesture from the commercial*) "Squish, squish, dip, dip?"

Alison Yes. But I don't play all the parts, just the Pixie. Shall we go to lunch? There won't be another show for quite a while. (*She rises and moves to him*)

Sandy Are you a good actress?

Alison Yes, I am.

Sandy A star?

Alison (*laughing at the idea*) No!

Sandy Are you going to be a star?

Alison (*after a brief pause*) No.

Sandy How do you know?

Alison I know.

Sandy How?

Alison (*shrugging*) I just know. I shall go from juvenile to character actress without ever having been a leading lady. It is my fate.

Sandy I don't understand that.

They are very close, and intent on each other, searching

Alison (*gently*) Maybe it's because you're an American. And a star?
Sandy (*shaking his head*) Business men don't have to be.
Alison Neither do actresses.
Sandy Don't you want to be a star?
Alison Yes.
Sandy Well, then?
Alison Do you get everything you want?
Sandy I try.

Her eyes flash with dismay for just a moment, and he sees it

I'm being rude again.
Alison No, it's all right. And please don't feel sorry for me. I'm not really a loser. I'm just not much of a winner, that's all. (*She smiles at him*) Shall we go to lunch?
Baldo (*briskly, having had enough*) Andiamo! (*He races up the* R *stairs*) It is dangerous to philosophize on an empty stomach.

Sandy and Alison move towards the L *stairs. Alison stops at the fountain*

Alison I love this fountain. Does it work? It has water in it.
Sandy No, it does not work. It is supposed to work. The hotel told me with great pride how old it is, and how much it cost to electrify it, and how much I would enjoy the play of the water—but it doesn't work.
Alison Where do you turn it on? (*She finds the switch*) Oh. (*She flicks it. Nothing happens*)
Baldo (*excusing it*) It is very old, and very beautiful . . .
Sandy It doesn't work.
Alison (*blithely*) Ah, well. Anyway, they did fix the phone. (*She starts up the stairs*) Where is the Piazza of Thingamabob?

Alison is half-way up the stairs. Sandy is just below her. Baldo is on the landing

Baldo Not far; we will walk. You have not been in Rome before?
Alison No.
Baldo (*to Sandy*) And you?
Sandy No.
Baldo Ah, I will have so much to show you!
Sandy (*emphatically*) We are not here as tourists!
Baldo No! No! No! No! But there is no harm to look. And when you are in Rome and you look, ah! I am sure your father will not mind; he loved Rome, yes? And he is comfortable, of this you can be sure. We take good care of the dead; better than the living.
Alison I think Mother would *like* me to have a look around, as long as I'm here.
Baldo Certo! It is spring! And you are in Rome for the first time! It is as though you were *born* for the first time. You are Adam! You are Eve! This is the Garden of Eden!
Alison And you are the serpent.
Baldo (*delighted*) Ecco!
Sandy (*amused*) What happens when we bite into the apple?

Baldo (*smiling at them blandly*) You lose your innocence. Non e vero?

And Sandy loses his smile, and neither one has an answer. Baldo gestures gracefully to the doors, and opens them

Please.

Sandy and Alison go out

Baldo looks down at the fountain in anger, and addresses the cupid sharply

Virgine Santa! You are a disgrace to Italy! Do something! Movite! (*He stamps the floor hard*)

The fountain lights up and starts to play

O.K.!

Baldo darts out of the room

The Lights dim down to blackness. Pause. The CURTAIN *remains up, as another kind of light slowly enters the room. The day is gone. It is night*

SCENE 2

The same. Late that night

The room is empty. Moonlight flows in from the terrace, but the room is quite dark

The telephone rings. It rings again. It rings again. It stops. Faintly, off in the corridor, we hear Alison singing, and then the voices of Sandy and Baldo join in, and the singing becomes louder as they approach

Alison
Sandy ⟨ "We three kings of Orient are. / Bearing gifts, we travel afar / Field and fountain, / Moor and mountain, / Following yonder star. / Ohhhhhhhhh . . ." ⟩ (*Singing off together*)
Baldo

The doors bang open and they enter, singing. Alison carries a silver tray, with three wine glasses. She has changed into a very pretty simple dress for dinner. Sandy carries a silver wine bucket from which protrudes a bottle of wine. Baldo carries the metal wine-bucket stand

Alison parades down the L *stairs, followed by Sandy. Baldo stops to close the doors, then parades down the* R *stairs. They keep singing*

"Star of wonder, star of night,
Star with royal beauty bright,

> Westward leading, still proceeding,
> Guide us to thy perfect . . ."

The telephone suddenly rings again sharply. They stop short, Sandy in the centre of the room, Alison to L of him, Baldo up R

Sandy The phone! Lights! (*He puts the wine bucket on the floor just below the sofa R and hurries towards the phone. He bumps into the desk stool*) Ow! Damn! (*He grabs the phone*) Hello! (*He turns on the desk lamp*)

During the above, Alison puts the tray on the armchair stool L, throws her handbag on to the armchair, and starts to search

Alison Where are they? (*She bumps into something*) Blast!
Baldo (*starting back up the stairs*) On the wall, yes? But where on the wall?
Sandy It's near the door! (*Into the phone*) Hello! Hello!
Baldo You say "Pronto!"
Alison (*near the bedroom*) This door here? (*She hits the radio switch*)

At the same time, Baldo, on the landing, finds a light switch

Baldo Ecco! Luce!

The chandelier and wall brackets light up. Alison lights a lamp, L, then transfers the wine glasses to the drinks table and puts the tray on the shelf below. The radio slowly fades in

Sandy Hello! . . . Yes, this is Mr Claiborne . . . Well, I'm here now; who was it? . . . Well, try to get them back, maybe they're still there.

Baldo lopes down the stairs to Sandy

Baldo (*offering to take the phone*) If you wish me to . . .

Sandy shakes his head

  Who is it?
Sandy America.
Baldo America! (*He crosses himself and turns away*)

The radio now comes alive, with a lilting Italian waltz. Alison starts to move with the music. Baldo wanders over to her and offers his arms. She accepts, and they start to waltz. They pause up R for a moment to turn on another lamp, then go on waltzing

Sandy (*during the above*) Hello! Hello! Oh! Diana! (*Rather guiltily*) Oh! How was the trip? I was out for dinner . . . (*He looks at his watch, and is appalled*) Well, you know they dine late in Rome. The service was slow . . . What? (*He is aware of the music now, and puts a hand over the mouthpiece and whispers frantically at the others*) Turn that off!
Baldo Where is it?
Alison I turned something on down there.
Sandy (*yelling*) What, Diana? (*Then, in a fierce whisper to the others*) Will you for Christ's sake turn that off! ! !
Baldo Ho! Trovato!

*Baldo turns the radio knob the wrong way, making the music roar for a
moment, then corrects himself and turns it off*

Sandy (*on the phone, still in the fierce whisper*) What, Diana? (*He catches
himself*) What? I mean, here? . . . Oh, with me! (*He looks at Alison*) Just
another guy. And hey, listen! We found Father! Yes! Father and—
Father! I got this great guy to help me. The Ambassador sent him over
just as you left . . . No, an Italian. And we went right out and found
Father; he's in a public morgue in an old part of Rome . . . Well, no, we
can't get him out, at least not right away, but we sure found him.

*Alison decides she will skip this tender family scene, and motions for per-
mission to go to the bathroom. Sandy waves her out*

   Alison goes, closing the door behind her

*Sandy sits on the stool next to the desk. Baldo wanders over and sits next to
him on the edge of the stool, where there is room, and leans his head against
Sandy's to listen*

   Drunk? No, I'm not drunk . . . No, we did not go out and celebrate, we
   merely had dinner . . . No, we did not get drunk! Do I have to tell you
   every move I make? . . . All right. We had lunch. We went out and
   searched. We found him. Then we separated for a while, and rejoined
   for dinner . . . No, we did not get drunk! . . . Of course I drank some
   wine! You have to drink wine in Italy, the water's no good, you know
   that . . . No, I can't get on a plane tonight, there's a lot of red tape to get
   through before we can get the body . . . (*Angrily*) Diana, it's so damned
   complicated! . . . All right, I'll give you an example, just one. I'm being
   sued for seven olive trees . . . Seven olive trees! When Father's car went
   down the mountain, it destroyed seven olive trees that belonged to a
   farmer named——

Baldo pulls out his notebook, opens it to the right page, and holds it out

   —Giuseppe Russo. He claims that they are the oldest and most historic
   olive trees in Italy, and he wants ten thousand dollars for them, or I
   can't move Father; he's got connections . . . No, I'm not making it up
   . . . Yes, I am trying to make a deal . . . No, I don't know when I'll get
   home. I may be here the rest of my life. Here, wait a minute, let him tell
   you.

*Baldo rises, takes a comb out of his pocket and combs his hair as he crosses
to the other side of Sandy to take the phone*

   My assistant Baldassare Pantaleone. And I'm not making that up,
   either! (*He shoves the whole telephone at Baldo*) Here! Tell her!

*Baldo takes the telephone. Sandy moves away angrily, emptying his lungs
with a great woosh of frustration*

Baldo (*smoothly*) Signora Claiborne, complimenti, you have a wonderful
husband . . . Just out to dinner . . . Yes, we had a charming dinner to-

gether, just we two. And let me assure you personally, Mrs Claiborne
. . . (*He is suddenly startled*) Eh? . . . What? Me?

Sandy returns and holds out his hand for the telephone

I have done nothing! (*He is suffering a severe attack from the other end*)
I mean, yes, I have done something! . . . Yes, I will try to do more! . . .
Yes, as fast as I can! . . . Yes, Mrs Claiborne! . . . Si, Mrs Claiborne! . . .
Yes, Mrs Claiborne, I will try! I promise! Promesso! Momento! ! (*He
shoves the telephone to Sandy in wide-eyed dismay*)

Sandy takes it, and sits on the stool again

Sandy Hello, Diana . . .

Baldo (*shaking a hand in amazement*) Madonna mia! (*He moves above the
desk to the wine stand that he had left by the* R *end of the sofa and picks it
up as Sandy continues to talk*)

Sandy Yes, dear . . . Yes, dear . . . Yes, dear . . . All right, I'm sorry I
shouted at you, but if you were here . . .

*Baldo, carrying the wine stand, starts towards the drinks table. As he comes
down around Sandy he pauses, then coolly bends down and kisses Sandy
nicely on the cheek. Then he moves happily away*

Diana, I'm doing the best I can . . . Well, I'll just keep sending cables, I
can't get a long-distance call out of here . . . (*And then he realizes that
something happened just a moment back. Did someone kiss him? He
looks around*)

Baldo has his back to him, and is innocently occupied with the wine

How's Mother? . . . How are the kids? . . . Give everybody my love . . .
Yes, dear . . . Yes, dear . . . Yes, dear . . . Good-bye. (*He hangs up, rises
and puts the telephone back on the desk, and heaves another heavy sigh of
frustration*)

Baldo moves easily towards him, with a grin

Baldo She is a strong woman, your wife.

Sandy glares at him

Let us have some wine.

Sandy I think I'll switch to whisky. (*He makes a strong, angry gesture*)
What is there about long-distance telephone calls?!

Baldo (*enjoying this*) We have a saying in Italy: when a man travels, he
should forget that he is married.

Sandy (*pointing to the phone*) How do you forget?

Baldo We have another saying: the only happy married men are deaf. (*He
comes up to Sandy and stands before him, and grins up at him impishly*)
Why did you get married?

Sandy Right at the moment, I couldn't tell you.

Baldo We also say about marriage: when you are young, not yet; when
you are old, why bother?

Sandy Do you keep a book of those?

Baldo I collect them for my Anglo-Saxon clients. (*He looks up at Sandy with a small, challenging smile*) Kiss me.
Sandy What?
Baldo Baci-me. Kiss me.
Sandy (*staring at him*) What's the matter with you?!
Baldo (*with a delighted whoop*) I love you! (*And he leaps up on Sandy and wraps his legs around Sandy's waist, and curls his arms around Sandy's neck, and starts chewing on one of Sandy's ears*)
Sandy (*struggling*) Listen! God damn it . . .!

They stagger about and Sandy finally manages to pry Baldo loose and push him off. Baldo lands on his feet with cat-like grace and stands there, grinning happily and cheerfully at Sandy

What the hell'd you do that for?
Baldo Don't you like me?
Sandy (*outraged*) I'm not that way!
Baldo You don't have to be.
Sandy I don't want to be.
Baldo (*advancing*) Ho! There is also an American saying: "If you haven't tried it, don't knock it." (*He stops before Sandy happily*) Kiss me.
Sandy (*backing away towards the desk, more startled than belligerent*) Now, stop that! Stop it! Cut it out! I ought to punch your head off!
Baldo (*grinning, and turning towards the drinks table*) I will get you some whisky.
Sandy I'll get it myself. (*He crosses below Baldo to the drinks table, pours himself a whisky, and goes back to the sofa*)

Baldo watches him, sweetly amused

Baldo Ah, Sandy—Mr Alexander Ben Claiborne—in a matter of this, you do not use your fists. This is love. You are a civilized man. Are you not curious?
Sandy (*sitting on the sofa*) Not a bit.
Baldo (*moving to him*) Let us send Alison away, and we will be together.

Baldo sits next to Sandy, and Sandy immediately springs to his feet and crosses to the armchair down L

Sandy Come on, why don't you go home?
Baldo (*joyously*) You mean you want to go to my place? (*He runs up the R stairs to the landing*)
Sandy No! ! ! ! (*He sits in the armchair and stretches his feet on the stool before him*)
Baldo (*on the landing; smoothly*) Ah, my Sandy—you are far from home, in another world. You are in Italy—my country—and that is something you have no idea of. Italy is an emotion. (*Without taking his eyes off Sandy, he reaches out and clicks the switch that turns off the chandelier and wall brackets. Then he starts smoothly down the stairs*) When a man comes to Italy, all the rules of his life are changed. Everything is new, everything is a delight. He can do anything, try anything. Self-indulgence is a way of life.

Sandy Not for me.

Baldo has reached the foot of the stairs, next to the standard lamp

Baldo Even for you. You are no different from the others who have come
to Italy in all the years, in all the centuries, and have been seduced. (*He
turns off the standard lamp, and now begins his smooth circle of the room
towards his objective, smoothly smiling and seductive, but really quite open
about it, and blithe and cheerful, almost merry. He moves towards the
sofa*) This is the place where sin is unknown as people think of it anywhere else. Man is a divine animal; all loves are pure. The god who
made Italy did not make the rest of the world, that was some other god.

*Baldo's words have a mesmerizing flow, and Sandy listens with amused
admiration as he drinks. And Baldo, as he goes, manages deftly and gently to
take off his jacket and drop it over the back of the sofa. He slowly moves
above Sandy*

Love, here, is unique and delicious, and all experiments have charm.
You have left your old life behind, all qualms and doubts behind. Be
free. Try something. Try anything. Try everything. (*He has now moved
just above Sandy*) Why think? Man must not think. He feels. (*He moves
past Sandy and turns off the lamp on the table behind him, then moves back
to him as he continues*) In Italy, in Rome, in the life we live, nothing is
sure. Only that you and I are here, that is sure. (*He sits on the stool,
facing Sandy, very close*) And if we make love, the moment of love is
sure, nothing else. So, love. (*He smiles with confident supplication*)

Sandy stares at him calmly

Sandy (*in matter-of-fact tones*) What a marvellous line to waste on another
man.

Baldo It is wasted on you?

Sandy Yes. Don't you ever think of anything but sex?

Baldo Don't you ever think how short life is?

Sandy And you're in a hurry.

Baldo Very much.

Sandy (*rising and turning*) Well, it's certainly a great line. If I'd had that
before I was married, I think I could have made every girl I met. (*He
switches on the lamp behind him and moves to the centre of the room*)

Baldo (*rising and following*) Oh, I use it on girls, too.

Sandy Successfully?

Baldo Mmm. But on a man it is more interesting. More difficult, but more
rewarding. So. Well?

Sandy Well?

Baldo (*grinning*) You are sure I cannot seduce you?

Sandy shakes his head

Perhaps if we dance . . .

Sandy (*retreating*) Look, you don't seem to understand. If it were a girl
who used that line on me . . .

Baldo You should not be so provincial.

Sandy I'm just a plain American boy.

Baldo I have known some plain American boys.

Sandy I'll bet you have.

Baldo Maybe tomorrow.

Sandy (*sitting*) The only thing I want to do tomorrow is get out of this country.

Baldo (*cheerfully*) O.K. Then I give it to you.

Sandy What?

Baldo The line: to use on her. Any of it, all of it.

Sandy (*surprised*) Alison?

Baldo Who else? Ho-ho! (*He puts on his jacket*) You cannot fool me. I have been watching you two all day.

Sandy What do you mean?

Baldo The way you look at each other? The feeling between you? I just thought maybe I could get to you before she did.

Sandy Thank you very much.

Baldo You do not find her attractive?

Sandy Well, yes, certainly, but . . .

Baldo Then take her! She wants you to!

Sandy Ah, come on!

Baldo Yes! She has told me!

Sandy When?

Baldo In the restaurant, when you went to the men's room.

Sandy stares at him, but Baldo's face is suffused with the light of truth, almost too suffused

Sandy I don't believe you.

Baldo (*reproachfully*) Sandy! You have not noticed? The way she looks at you? The little things she does? You want to prove it? O.K., I will leave you. (*He darts up the stairs to the landing*)

Sandy Wait a minute! !

Baldo (*coming right back down the other stairs*) You want me to stay!

Sandy (*anxiously*) Well, don't go yet.

Baldo You think maybe the three of us could get something going? (*He considers*) No, she is too English. Still, these days, the English . . .

Sandy What the hell's the matter with you? First you try to make me, then you want me to make her, now you think maybe the three of us— haven't you got any morals at all?

Baldo (*strongly*) We must not waste the night! That is the true morality.

Sandy Don't you ever just go to sleep?

Baldo Madonna mia! (*Pleading*) Sandy, please, everything I tell to you is true. You have stepped out of your world, you are free. And she is free. You are in space. There are no rules. There is no one to see you, no one to stop you, whatever you want to do, you can do. You want to make love, she wants to be loved, it can happen! Let it happen! You are alone in Rome. Whenever again will you have a night like this? Let it happen!

The bedroom door opens, and Alison appears looking neat and lovely

Sandy rises

Alison That is the biggest bathroom I have ever seen in my life! Waterloo Station!

Baldo Good-bye. (*He races up the stairs to the landing*)

Alison Where are you going?

Baldo To an orgy.

Alison Ho! Take me along!

Baldo Not tonight. But next time we have ladies' night, I'll let you know. A domani.

Alison Ah, well . . . (*With a happy yelp*) Ciao!

Baldo (*slightly disgusted*) Ah, no! No! You do not say it that way.

Alison What?

Baldo Ciao. It is not—(*he does a bright little skip and gesture*)—"cheerio!" It is a gentle word. (*Gently and slowly*) Ciao. It is a word we use when someone is going far away for a long time, and we may never see him again. And so we say it gently—slowly—quietly—often twice . . .

Alison is drawn across the room to him and stands below, looking up at him

Alison (*moved, smiling*) Yes, I see. Ciao—ciao . . .

Baldo (*with an approving gesture*) That. (*He nods to her, smiling*) Ciao . . . (*He looks over at Sandy with a glint of a mocking grin*) Ciao . . .

Baldo goes out

A moment, then Alison turns back to Sandy, and notices that half the lights are out

Alison He is a charmer, isn't he?

Sandy Bewitching.

Alison Did he make a pass at you while I was in the loo?

Sandy nods

Yes, I thought he would. Did you knock him down?

Sandy No.

Alison That's good. So many men think they have to. (*She grins at him with amused enquiry*)

Sandy No, I didn't make a date, either.

Alison I didn't think you would.

Neither can think of anything more to say. But then they are saved by the bells of Rome, which begin to toll and chime everywhere in the city. Alison is delighted

The bells of Rome! Listen! (*She listens with tightly shut eyes, then opens them and smiles at him*) Baldo says there are four hundred and fifty-six churches in Rome.

Sandy I'd swear it was four hundred and fifty-seven.

Alison Don't you like them?

Sandy Yes, I do.

They smile at each other, and the constraint returns. Alison decides to break it. She moves to get her handbag

Alison Well, home to the hovel.

Sandy (*quickly*) Have a drink!

Alison (*stopping and hesitating*) Are you on whisky?

He nods

> I think I will have a touch more of that lovely wine. No, I'll do it. (*She takes the bottle out of the wine bucket, and glances casually at the chandelier*) What happened to the lights?

Sandy Baldo turned them off.

Alison (*grinning*) To put you in the mood?

Sandy Would you like me to turn them on?

Alison No, it's all right, I can see.

He stares at her, very much stirred. Baldo has had the desired effect. Alison studies the wine label. The bells begin to fade

> "Est! Est! Est!" Only the Italians would name a wine, "This is it! This is it! This is it!" What was that story Baldo told us about it?

Sandy About the Pope who sent a monk all through Italy to find the nicest white wine of the country.

Alison This is it. He sent the right monk. (*She pours a glass, replaces the bottle, and carries her drink across to him*) I didn't thank you for dinner. Thank you for dinner. Such a good dinner.

Sandy We did have fun, didn't we?

Alison It was super. (*She sits on the sofa*)

Sandy goes to refill his drink. The bells are silent

Sandy I think Baldo's the only guy I've ever known who could make a festival out of looking for two dead people. Did you have twinges?

Alison Of guilt? Mmmm. Waves of guilt. And then thinking: Mother wouldn't mind; she'd have liked it, in fact. Baldo was right. You carry your tears in your pocket.

Sandy returns above the sofa towards the desk

Sandy Do you think he'll get everything finished tomorrow?

Alison Well, he certainly got us off to a flying start, didn't he? We found the bodies, and managed to get in a bit of sight-seeing, too. (*She sighs blissfully*) The Sistine Chapel. It was lovely seeing the Sistine Chapel.

Sandy Yes. I'm beginning to like Rome.

Alison Oh, I love it.

Sandy fiddles with papers on the desk, and stares at her self-consciously

Sandy He did say the toughest part is still to come.

Alison Baldo?

Sandy (*nodding*) The papers—the permissions—the releases . . .

Alison You mustn't worry. I'm sure you'll be on your way home to-morrow.

Sandy You, too.

Alison (*nodding*) Back to London.

Sandy I'm not sure I want to be, now.

Alison Why?

Sandy Because of you.

Alison Don't be silly.

Sandy (*moving closer to the sofa*) I keep wondering if I'll ever see you again.

Alison (*brightly*) Of course! In films, when I'm a star. And you'll point to me and say, "I knew her once. We were in Rome together, with our parents."

Sandy That's not what I mean.

Alison Well, if I become a big star, I'll probably go to America to make personal appearances. You can come and see me. Bring the children.

Sandy That's not what I mean, either.

Alison (*amused*) If you ever come to London, give me a ring.

Sandy I don't know when that would happen.

Alison Nonsense, all Americans come to London sooner or later, to see the changing of the guard.

Sandy takes a gulp of whisky, and puts his glass on the table behind the sofa. Alison, seeming not to notice, puts her glass on the floor under the sofa, very casually, Sandy sits down abruptly on the sofa

Sandy Alison . . .

Alison (*giving way a bit*) Mmmmmm?

Sandy It has been a wonderful day. And I feel as though I've known you— practically for ever.

Alison That's flattering.

Sandy Do you have that feeling?

Alison That I've known you for ever? Mmmmmm—no. But I do think we've become friends.

He takes her by the shoulders and turns her to him

Sandy Oh, much more, Alison. Much, much more. (*And he tries to kiss her, quite clumsily*)

Dismayed by his clumsiness, she pushes him off

Alison No, don't do that.

Sandy slips off the sofa and lands on the floor, flat on his back, and lies there, suffused with embarrassment

(*Rising, alarmed*) Are you all right?

Sandy (*grimly*) I'm just dandy.

Alison I'm sorry, I really am. But you did take it for granted, didn't you?

Sandy (*rising*) No.

Alison Yes, you did.

He picks up her glass and hands it to her

Sandy Well, you did put your glass down.

Alison I had a presentiment you were going to spill it all over me.

Sandy I probably would have.

Alison You're not very good at that sort of thing, are you?

Sandy No.

Alison You do show a frightful lack of practice.

Sandy I hardly ever try.

Alison Isn't that curious.

Sandy What?

Alison This morning you told me your father wasn't the kind that makes passes at strange women, now you tell me that you're not. Do you come of a long line of monks?

Sandy I just haven't got the guts, that's all. (*He retrieves his drink and goes to add a splash to it*) Boy, that didn't take long.

Alison (*sitting on the sofa; amused*) Don't tell me you're fundamentally shy?

Sandy (*returning to the centre of the room*) Yes. And scared.

Alison Of what? Your wife?

Sandy Of being caught, of being laughed at. When I consider making a pass at a girl, the thought always crosses my mind that she'll slap my face and tell my wife, and then the two of them will get together and have a big laugh. And I'm stopped before I get started.

Alison It didn't stop you just now. I might tell your wife.

Sandy My wife is four thousand miles away, and I defy you to get her on that telephone. (*And, quite depressed, he wanders to the armchair he was in when Baldo tried to seduce him*)

Alison looks across at him with delight, hugely enjoying the situation, and liking him more than ever

Alison Ah, but then that's it, isn't it? Faithfulness is a matter of geography, and you've only the courage of being away.

Sandy (*sitting; morosely*) Don't rub it in. I know I'm square.

Alison And then, too, you probably felt strangely confident this time, didn't you? (*No answer*) Didn't you?

He grimaces uncomfortably

Because Baldo, the Old Serpent himself, probably suggested that I was susceptible and willing. (*No answer*) Didn't he?

He nods sadly. She rises, bright with inner glee, and like Baldo before her, she begins to circle the room smoothly, wickedly, working her way towards him

And you believed him. And you thought: well, why not? For Baldo, the Devil, said: here you are, far from home, in another country, Italy, no less! And here is a girl who wants to be loved, and you may never see her again. Take her! Be free! (*Having circled the sofa, she reaches the L side of the room. During the following she moves down to him smoothly, and circles around the back of his chair with wicked grace*) Italy is an emotion, and self-indulgence is a way of life. When you come to Italy from another part of the world, all the rules of your life are changed. The god who made Italy did not make the rest of the world; that was another god.

His head comes up a little as he hears the echoes, and he wonders

Take her. Nothing in life is sure. Only that if you make love, that moment of love is sure. So love! (*She has now come fully around him, and stands above him towards the centre of the room, playing it with grace and*

charm and full enjoyment) You are alone in Rome, let it happen. Whenever again will you have a night like this? Let it happen!
Sandy (*aghast*) When did he say all that to you?
Alison At the restaurant, when you went to the loo.
Sandy Well, he is consistent. (*He shakes his head ruefully*) I get the feeling
from Baldo that the Italians only discovered sex yesterday, and they
can't wait to get at it. With whatever happens to be in the way.

*Alison looks at him for a moment, then drifts across the room away from
him, pensively, and comes to a stop near the sofa, with her back to him*

Alison (*simply*) But that doesn't make what he said untrue, does it? (*She
waits*) The trouble with the Devil is, he tells the most seductive truths.

*And Sandy, startled and hopeful, comes alive. He rises, leaving his glass on
the floor, and moves to her, then stops behind her, not sure of himself*

Sandy Alison . . .
Alison (*not turning*) And there are ways and ways of asking.

It takes him only a moment to find the magic word

Sandy (*tenderly*) Permesso?

She smiles gratefully, and turns to him

Alison Avanti!

He takes her in his arms, and kisses her. She laughs lovingly

Est! Est! Est!
Sandy Permesso?

*Holding her, he guides her down to the sofa, and they sit facing each other.
They lean forward to kiss again; the telephone rings. They look at it. It keeps
ringing. Sandy rises quickly, steps across to the desk, and jumps hard on the
floor. The phone ringing cuts off. He turns to Alison with a proud grin of
accomplishment*

It works both ways.
Alison Aren't the Italians clever?

*Sandy takes off his jacket, feeling marvellously confident, now. He drapes
the jacket over the phone, and reaches over and snaps off the desk light as he
begins to talk*

Sandy When you come to Italy, all the rules of your life are changed. (*He
has fallen into the seductive smoothness that Baldo started and that Alison
carried on, and he finds it suits him very well. He turns back to the sofa*)
The god who made Italy did not make the rest of the world; that was
another god. (*He sits on the sofa again, and she leans back, and he
stretches out with her, amorously*) Love, here, is unique and delicious.
Whenever again will you have a night like this? Let it happen.
Alison (*with a happy sigh*) Oh, you're better than Baldo!

Sandy and Alison kiss, as—

the CURTAIN *falls*

ACT II

SCENE 1

The same. Early afternoon, several days later

There has been a remarkable, colourful change in the room: it is now filled to overflowing with flowers. There are spring flowers everywhere. And the sun pours into the room

When the CURTAIN *rises, John Wesley is at the telephone, looking eager and anxious*

Wesley Hello, pronto! Pronto! . . . Signore Simonelli? . . . Oh, scusate tanto. Hello, pronto! . . . Signore Simonelli? . . . Ah! Io e John Wesley della United States Embassy. Recorda? . . . What (*He winces*) Do you parlate Inglese? . . . Thank God . . . Yes, the United States Embassy. I am calling on behalf of one of our citizens, Mr Alexander Claiborne, remember? . . . Good. (*With pleased self-importance*) Well. Now. The problem is this. We are trying to get an export licence for Mr Claiborne's father . . . Yes . . . He doesn't want to export anything, we want to export him . . . Hello! Hello! Pronto! (*He stares at the phone for a moment, then puts it down sadly*) Ah, jiminy. (*He picks up the phone again*) The United States Embassy, per favore. (*He waits*)

The front door bangs open, and a beautiful apparition appears in the doorway: a great, moving mass of spring flowers. A leg beneath it kicks the door shut

Wesley looks over, startled, but the telephone brings him back to attention

Hello, this is John Wesley; give me Mr Botts.

The moving bouquet staggers down the steps and into the room. The motivating force is, of course, Alison

Hello, Mr Botts, Wesley. I haven't been able to . . . What? . . . What? . . . What do you mean?

And at this moment, Alison starts to stumble, tries to recover, wavers, begins to lose flowers, and grabs for them

Alison (*loudly*) Help!
Wesley (*on the phone*) Just a minute, Mr Botts, I'll be right back.

He races to help Alison, but miscalculates his speed and runs into her. He keeps her upright, but all the flowers fall to the ground. Alison looks fresh and dewy in a blouse and skirt, and wears a big, floppy, flowered straw hat on the back of her head

Alison Ahhhhh!

Sandy hurries in from the bedroom, shutting the door

Wesley I'm awfully sorry, excuse me. (*He races back to the phone*)
Sandy What happened?
Alison I was trying to make an entrance.
Sandy My God, Alison, you haven't bought more flowers!
Alison I can't help it, it's like eating peanuts.

They both go down on their hands and knees to gather up the flowers

Wesley (*at the same time, on the phone*) Hello, Mr Botts, what were you saying? . . . Well, what's it about? . . . Yes, sir . . . Yes, sir . . . Yes, sir, right away. (*He hangs up, goes to the sofa, picks up his hat and briefcase, and hurries up the stairs*) I'm awfully sorry about that. Excuse me.

Sandy rises and moves to the foot of the stairs

Sandy Hey, where are you going?
Wesley Back to the Embassy. It's got something to do with you.
Sandy What?
Wesley I don't know, but you've suddenly become very important.
Alison It's about time.
Sandy Wait a minute!
Wesley I'll call you as soon as I know.

And Wesley is gone, slamming the door

Sandy Now what the hell?
Alison Let nature take its course. Would you mind helping me, please?

Sandy goes back to help her gather the flowers

Sandy Do you think they got the papers signed?
Alison I sincerely hope not. I don't want to leave Rome, ever!
Sandy (*piling the flowers back into her arms*) Alison, you've got to stop this flower kick.
Alison But they don't cost anything.
Sandy What do you mean, they don't cost anything?
Alison Only lire.
Sandy Oh, God.

Alison's arms are filled with flowers again. He hands her the last flower

Alison Thank you. Well? You might kiss me.

He parts the flowers and kisses her

(*Sniffing enthusiastically*) Mmmm! You smell marvellous.

Sandy (*laughing*) It couldn't be the flowers. Where are you going to put them?

Alison In the bath.

Sandy You've already got flowers in the bathtub.

Alison But such a big bathtub. Room for all.

Sandy (*embracing her again, from behind*) I know. First time I ever took a bath with daffodils.

Alison And an English bird, all at once? (*She giggles*) There's something sort of decadent about two people in a bath. Especially with flowers. Baldo would approve.

Sandy And I'll bet Baldo could think of something to do with a daffodil that nobody else has ever thought of.

Alison laughs and starts for the bedroom, then stops short

Alison Oh. Cable for you. Right hand pocket.

For a moment they both look anxious; trouble in Paradise. Then Sandy reaches into her pocket and gets the cable. He reads it

Sandy (*reading, in matter-of-fact tones*) "Congratulations, you are a grandfather."

Alison (*nodding soberly*) How old are your children?

Sandy Ten and eleven.

Alison It must be all that orange juice you Americans drink. (*She heads for the bedroom*) Who's it for?

Sandy Mr Bernstein.

Alison Poor man, he's probably been on edge all day, waiting to hear. Is it a boy or a girl?

Sandy (*looking at the cable again*) Boy.

Alison (*as she goes*) How nice! His first grandson!

Alison exits to the bedroom

Sandy How do you . . . (*Then he grins*) Guess you're right. (*He picks up the phone*) Give me the—portiere . . . Hi, portiere, this is Mr Claiborne in the royal suite. I got a cable here by mistake, it's for a Mr Bernstein. Will you send up for it, please? . . . You're welcome. (*He hangs up, puts the cable under the phone, and calls*) Alison!

Alison (*off*) Won't be a minute!

Sandy Do you know how many lire there are in a pound?

Alison (*off*) Haven't the foggiest.

Sandy One thousand, five hundred and seventeen!

Alison enters

Alison Wow! Imagine having all that! (*She closes the bedroom door behind her and comes part way towards him, smiling*)

Sandy Lire! Not pounds!

Alison I know, darling, but it does seem a lot of money, doesn't it? Do I set your teeth on edge? Do I outrage the Harvard Business School in you?

Sandy (*lying down on the sofa*) Well, it's your money. But I do think you
ought to know what you're spending.
Alison Oh, I think it's much more important to know what you're buying!
(*She takes command of the stage*) Ah, my darling, what's money? Here
we are in Rome, in love, we're having a thing—and the two don't always
go together—and I can fill my arms with flowers for ten bob. You see,
I do know what I paid.
Sandy Are you?
Alison What?
Sandy In love.
Alison If you don't know by now . . .! Music (*She turns on the radio*)

*The room is immediately filled with Italian dance music with a rocking beat
Alison kicks off her shoes, and starts to dance with charming abandon*

Come on, dance with me!

*He shakes his head and watches her with amused affection as she dances
across the room to the desk, plucks a rose from a vase on the desk, and waves
it as she dances up behind the sofa towards the fountain*

Ah, please! Don't be a drag! You danced with me last night. (*She dances
on the edge of the fountain*)

Sandy sits up and turns to look at her

Sandy I do so love you!
Alison Do you? Really? (*She runs up the L stairs and dances happily at the
top, waving her rose*) Sometimes I think you do, and then I think, "Don't
be a twit, he's just having a thing, and Baldo was right. He's just taking
advantage of Italy and your sentimental nature." Do you really? Love
me?
Sandy (*rising to face her*) Yes! ! ! !
Alison Then dance with me! (*She tosses him the rose and races down to him*)

*He puts the rose between his teeth and puts his arms around her, and they
dance down to the front of the stage. Suddenly the music stops short. Alison
looks round*

What happened to the music?
Sandy Somebody, somewhere in this hotel, stamped his foot.

*He tosses the rose away, and kisses her hard, holding her close, and brings
her down to the floor slowly, she waving a hand in protest. They lie on the
floor in a deep embrace. Finally, Alison manages to come up for air*

Alison Sandy, not here! Really! On the floor? When we've got that great
big beautiful bed in there?

They sit up and lean against each other, with the sofa behind them

Sandy Ah, that great big beautiful bed in there.
Alison (*dreamily, happily*) Mmmm. Our "letto matrimoniale". That's the
nicest Italian phrase I've learned. "Our marriage bed."
Sandy (*dreamily*) It's the way all beds should be: big enough for a search,
small enough for a find.

Alison (*dreamily*) Aren't the Italians wise? How can anything go wrong when they've got a bed like that?

Sandy decides to opt for action, and tries to pick her up

Sandy Let's try it and see if you're right.

Alison (*stopping him*) Not now. No. (*She looks at him adoringly*) Ah, Sandy, you really are something special. It makes me want to do all sorts of spectacular things for you.

Sandy (*interested*) Can you?

Alison I haven't been very inventive, have I? Just a simple, healthy, normal girl.

Sandy They're the best kind.

Alison No, I should do better. (*Being severe with herself*) Yes, I should. When two people fall into an affair like this, the girl in the case is supposed to be skilful, and deft, and full of all kinds of imaginative tricks, and the man in the case is supposed to be amazed, and say he's never known anyone like her.

Sandy (*enjoying that*) I've never known anyone like you.

Alison But I don't amaze you.

Sandy You amaze me every minute of the day.

Alison I'm talking about night.

Sandy (*tenderly, laughing*) You're such a fool.

Alison I know. But it's going to be all right now, you'll see. Walking home from the Spanish Steps just now, with the flowers, I made all sorts of plans for tonight, and I've got some marvellous ideas—if I can just keep my nerve.

Sandy Let's try them now.

He attacks her; she fights him off

Alison No, I'm not ready!

Sandy While they're fresh in your mind!

Alison No! Down, boy!

She tries to fight him off, but he has her this time, and gets her down flat on her back on the floor and lies on top of her and kisses her

   (*Murmuring feebly*) You're not giving me—much chance—to manoeuvre
   . . .

Holding her tightly, Sandy rolls over so that his back is now on the floor and she is lying on top of him

Sandy How's that?

Alison Much better.

Sandy Permesso? (*He slips his hand under her blouse*)

Alison (*laughing*) Permesso? (*She lifts the bottom of his shirt*)

Waiter (*off*) Permesso?

Alison Oh, my God!

She scrambles off Sandy, who remains lying outstretched, flat on his back, with a look of contentment on his face

You lecher! Sandy! Cover yourself up!

Waiter (*off, knocking*) Permesso?

Alison Momento! (*She pulls at her skirt, rearranges herself neatly, and sits on the sofa to put on her shoes. Then, with lady-like grace*) Avanti!

The door opens, the Waiter enters and comes directly down into the room

Waiter Scusi . . . (*He comes down to where Sandy is lying and smiles down at him, politely*)

Alison Sandy!

Sandy does not move

Waiter (*smiling down at the prone body*) Signore Claiborne? You have una telegramma?

Sandy Oh! Yeah. (*He points to the table*)

The Waiter goes and gets the telegram

Waiter Grazie. (*He starts to move back*)

Alison (*rising, brightly*) Just a minute! Momento! (*To Sandy*) Have you got any money?

Sandy (*handing her a wad of bank-notes*) It's only lire.

Alison (*moving to the Waiter*) Giorgio, how do you say "best wishes"?

Waiter Come?

Alison You know—"*best!—wishes!*"

Waiter Ah! "Auguri!"

Alison "Auguri!" I like that. (*She gives him some money*) Here. You tell Mr Bernstein "auguri" from the people in the royal suite.

Waiter Ah, si! From Signora and Signore Claiborne.

Alison (*blithely*) Well, if you want to put it that way. (*She forks over the rest of the money*) You have all the right instincts.

Waiter Grazie tanto.

Alison Prego. Is that right?

Waiter (*who adores her*) Molto bene! Benissimo!

The Waiter hurries up the stairs and goes out

Alison turns and looks to Sandy for approval. He still lies on the floor

Sandy What'd you give him?

Alison It's only lire. (*Moving to the windows*) After all, it's "auguri" for Mr Bernstein. What a lovely word. I must learn Italian. (*She looks down at the street, and stretches out her hand and declaims romantically*) "Divieto di sosta!"

Sandy (*sitting up*) What does that mean?

Alison No parking. (*She turns back to Sandy and indicates the Waiter who has gone*) Do you really think he thinks I'm Mrs Claiborne? Doesn't he remember your wife?

Sandy (*rising and moving to her*) From the way you've been tipping him, he prefers to think you're Mrs Claiborne.

Alison What about the Manager of the hotel, and the Assistant Manager, and all that? Since I moved in?

Sandy (*putting his arms round her*) They don't seem to notice, as long as they're getting the full rate on the room.
Alison (*affronted*) Are they charging you for me?
Sandy Of course.
Alison Hmmm! The wages of sin. Where were we?
Sandy On the floor. (*He picks her up and carries her downstage*)
Alison No, no, the spell's broken.
Sandy (*putting her down*) Sure?
Alison Maybe later, when we're changing for dinner.

Sandy grins, then looks at her seriously

Sandy Sit down. (*He leads her to the sofa*) I want to talk to you.
Alison What about?
Sandy Sit down.

They sit. He stares at her grimly

What are we going to do?

Alison immediately raises her hand in a traffic cop gesture

Alison Oh, no! None of that! We agreed: we weren't going to talk about that.
Sandy But Alison . . .

Alison rises quickly to her feet and takes a dramatic stand

Alison No! Absolutely not! (*She dramatizes it*) "God knows I didn't want to fall in love with you! What are we to do? I am a married man, with two children and a Lincoln Continental!" None of that stuff. (*She moves away down* L)
Sandy But I have to talk to you!
Alison Why? What difference would it make? You're not contemplating divorce, are you?
Sandy I don't know.
Alison Don't be silly.
Sandy Well, then, what?
Alison Nothing.
Sandy You mean . . .? (*He makes a great, parting gesture with his hands and arms, sweeping the two of them apart*)
Alison I mean exactly—(*and she copies the gesture*)—I'll take the high road and you take the low road, and I'll be in London before you get to St Louis, and the chances of our ever meeting in Scotland are very dim indeed.
Sandy And that's it.
Alison That is it. (*She runs to him and kneels on the sofa next to him*) Ah, my darling, think what we've had. We expected one night, we've had four. That's four thousand per cent profit, isn't it? Or is it four hundred?
Sandy You said you loved me.
Alison I do. But the world's not black and white, and there isn't always an answer.
Sandy There has to be.

Alison No, I can think of hundreds of questions . . . (*She smiles*) Besides—
when we were wandering through all those government offices with
Baldo yesterday, I talked to an assistant secretary of an assistant
assistant, and he said we may be stuck here for months. Isn't that
lovely?

Sandy Except by that time my whole family'll turn up.

Alison Oh, that's no problem. I'll move to another floor. And we'll nod
politely when we meet in the lobby. And you'll get Baldo to take your
wife to see the Sistine Chapel while you sneak round to make love to me.

He stares at her, trying not to laugh

Does that sound immoral?

Sandy (*lovingly laughing*) Yes.

Alison Yes, it does, rather, doesn't it? But the world is so at sixes and
sevens that we *have* got to live every moment, don't you think? Vora-
ciously? Taking what we can get? Licking up every crumb?

Sandy (*adoring her*) I don't know how to let you go.

Alison You'll find a way. (*She looks away with a wry smile, thoughtfully,
and speaks half to herself*) It *is* strange, coming full circle like this.

Sandy Full circle like what?

Alison looks at him, and decides

Alison My mother, your father; you and me.

Sandy You think they would have disapproved of this.

Alison I can't think why, since they did it themselves.

Sandy Who?

Alison Who do you think? Did it never occur to you that they might have
been lovers?

Sandy Lovers? Who?

Alison Who do you think?

Sandy Your mother and my fa . . . Don't be an ass. (*He rises and moves to
the drinks table*)

Alison (*outraged*) Oh! ! You're the ass! I wanted to tell you the first day
we met, but you were being so grand I didn't have the nerve. (*She rises
to her feet and does an imitation of him being grand and stuffy*) "Oh, they
must have met accidentally in Florence or Perugia in a shop or hotel,
the way tourists do!" Do you know when they met accidentally in
Florece or Perugia in a shop or hotel? Twelve years ago!

Sandy You're out of your mind.

Alison (*dismissing him, turning up towards the windows*) O.K., they were
strangers, absolute strangers. (*She sings soulfully*) "Take my hand, I'm
a stranger in paradise . . ."

Sandy (*moving back* C) Now, wait a minute. What the hell are you talking
about?

Alison Nothing. I'm a stranger here myself. Stuffed shirt. (*And she
marches past him, hurling the epithet in his face as she goes*)

Sandy Alison! Tell me!

Alison I told you!

Sandy I don't believe you!

Alison O.K. ! ! !

Sandy Your mother and my father met twelve years ago?

Alison Yes.

Sandy Where?

Alison Here in Italy.

Sandy And fell in love?

Alison Yes. Even as you and I.

Sandy How do you know?

Alison She told me.

Sandy What happened when they met?

Alison They travelled together. For a month.

Sandy And then what?

Alison They decided they liked it.

Sandy And so?

Alison They did it again.

Sandy The following year?

Alison Yes.

Sandy And they kept on meeting from then on? For one month every year?

Alison Yes.

Sandy stares at her and considers

Sandy (*smoothly*) But not the same month every year.

She glares at him, seeing the trap

Alison Yes. May. Don't be clever. It was always the month of May. "In the spring, an old man's fancy." Well? What month of the year did your father go to Italy? Every year? To get away from his family?

Sandy (*with dazed admiration and pride*) Why, the clever son-of-a-bitch.

Alison (*sitting on the armchair stool*) You took the words out of my mouth.

Sandy How do you like that? My father! Joseph T. Claiborne!

Alison The pride of St Louis.

Sandy (*excited and stirred*) That quiet, proper, conventional man! Why, he wouldn't even take a drink until six in the evening. And all that time —for twelve years—he had a mistress!

Alison My darling mother.

Sandy And nobody knew. Not even me. He used to tell us he was going to Italy for a rest. Some rest! (*He crows delightedly*) Ho! ! ! (*Then, abruptly*) Did they ever see each other at any other time?

Alison No.

Sandy No. It's perfect. (*He circles the room*) One month a year. May. To meet fresh every year in the spring, and go wandering together through Italy—hand in hand—free and idyllic—no one to see you, no one to know. What a way to live! (*Having circled the room, he is back in the centre*)

His glance falls on Alison, but she does not take it a bit impersonally

Alison Oh, no! Don't you get any ideas!

She picks up a cushion from the armchair and charges at him. He backs away, raising his hands in defence

Sandy No, darling, I didn't mean it that way!

Alison Like hell you didn't! (*She strikes at him wildly*)

Sandy Alison, I swear! I wouldn't ask you to do a thing like that!

Alison Like hell you wouldn't! (*She keeps trying to hit him*)

He grabs the cushion from her

Sandy Now, wait, wait, wait. Tell me more.

Alison (*breaking away*) That's all. It made me so furious!

Sandy Why? You mean it's all right for you to have an affair, but not your mother?

Alison Yes! No! That's not the point! Why didn't he marry her? He didn't love your mother. He said he didn't.

Sandy (*wincing as he thinks back*) No—they hadn't been in love for years. But they got along, the way people do. (*He tosses the cushion into the armchair*)

Alison What a horrible thought. Better to have left her.

Sandy It isn't that easy, love. For a man like that. I think he could have left his wife. It was his world he couldn't leave.

Alison Rubbish.

Sandy Did your mother expect him to marry her?

Alison No. She kept saying that she was better off with that one month a year than most women with twelve.

Sandy (*moving to her*) Ah! Then why do you resent it?

Alison Because it was wrong for her! She *should* have married again. But once she met your father, she took it for granted that she would be faithful to him—(*she is quite surprised to find that she is about to cry*)—and she was—until death. (*And she bursts into tears and goes into his arms*)

Sandy (*holding her*) Come on, now.

Alison (*against his breast*) She was such a fool!

Sandy She was happy, wasn't she?

Alison (*muffled*) Yes.

Sandy Well, then?

Alison You don't understand!

There is a knock at the door. Alison breaks away and stalks up towards the windows

Baldo walks in. He is terribly worried, and wears as psychological protection the dark sunglasses that are part of every young Italian's equipment

Baldo Permesso? What is the matter?

Alison (*grimly*) He wants me to be European representative of the Claiborne-Missouri Tool Company.

Baldo What's wrong with that?

Alison I don't have to sell any tools.

Sandy (*irritated*) Ah, come on, Alison!

Alison (*stentorianly*) That's all! ! ! ! (*She stares out of the window at Rome*)

Baldo comes down into the room

Sandy Baldo, where have you been?
Baldo Working.
Sandy (*impatiently*) Well, what's happening?
Baldo Nothing. (*Troubled*) May I have a whisky?
Sandy Help yourself. But you've still got the rest of the afternoon. Isn't there anyone you can get to? Do you need some more money? Look, Baldo, you've been great fun, but you haven't got us anywhere since last Friday.
Alison (*turning back into the room abruptly*) That's not fair. He's had us all over Rome.

Baldo carries his drink across to the desk and sits on the stool

Sandy I know, but . . .
Alison (*moving above the sofa*) You saw yourself how impossible it is. All those petty little functionaries. You walk into an office, and the man behind the desk starts shaking his head before you've opened your mouth. (*She demonstrates*) What *is* that, Baldo?
Baldo (*ruefully*) It is the official Italian greeting.
Sandy All right, all right. Baldo, I'll get you some more money. (*He dashes towards the bedroom*) I don't give a damn if you have to bribe the entire government of Italy!

Sandy exits to the bedroom

Baldo (*calling after him loudly*) They will not take a bribe unless it is in an envelope!
Alison Well?
Baldo (*sadly*) We haven't got that many envelopes.
Alison Baldo, what's the matter?

Baldo shrugs hopelessly, takes off his dark glasses, and lays them on the table

Baldo (*sadly*) My mother always wanted me to be a priest.

Sandy breezes in with a thick package of 500-lire notes

Sandy O.K., Baldo, here. Hit 'em where they live! (*He goes to Baldo*)

Alison sits on the armchair stool to watch

Baldo Ah, no—no . . .
Sandy You said yourself bribery keeps the machinery moving.
Baldo It is moving, believe me. So much money!
Sandy Look, learn something from an American business man. If you've got the power, use it. This stuff is power.
Baldo (*pushing the money away*) No, you are already too much generous. I will solve my own problems. (*He has a new thought, and leaps to his feet*) Sandy! I have a proposition to make to you! Why do you not have your father buried here in Rome? (*To Alison*) And your mother! Yes, here in Rome! (*He moves back and forth between the two of them en-*

thusiastically) You have never seen an Italian funeral? Ah, it is so beautiful! More beautiful than a wedding! All black and gold with carriages, and the horses wear feathers. And the flowers, Alison, the flowers! And all Rome will come to honour your father and mother, I will see to it. The Pope will come! The Pope himself will come! (*He gives the benediction, then has a thought*) Ah, they were not Catholics. Then he will send a Cardinal. Sandy, let us do this!

Sandy (*staring at him*) What's the matter with you?

Baldo Your father loved Italy, so. And they were lovers, yes? I believe they were lovers. Let us bury the lovers together. It will be beautiful.

Sandy Are you out of your mind? What's happened?

Baldo stares at Sandy mutely, agonized

Baldo, what's happened?

Alison (*moving to them*) What is it, Baldo?

Sandy (*fiercely*) Baldo, what's happened now?

Baldo (*simply*) The bodies have disappeared.

Sandy (*staggered*) The bodies have what?

Alison Disappeared?

Baldo nods miserably

Sandy (*aghast*) How—could bodies—disappear?

Baldo I wish I knew.

Sandy grabs hold of him roughly

Sandy God damn it, what the hell have you done?

Alison (*quickly apprehensive*) Sandy!!

The telephone rings. Sandy lets go of Baldo and dashes to it

Baldo, what did happen?

Baldo (*wandering away*) Madonna mia, how I wish I knew.

Sandy (*on the phone*) Hello?... Yes!... Oh, John, yes! (*Aside to Alison*) John Wesley at the Embassy. (*Into the phone; amazed*) You have? You've got them?

Baldo The bodies?

Sandy Signed? All signed? (*To Alison*) The papers are signed. (*Into the phone*) How'd you do it?... From Washington? Who phoned from Washington?... No kidding! (*To Alison*) Hey! The Italian Ambassador in Washington phoned the Foreign Minister here. (*Into the phone*) But how did it happen? Who did it? Who pulled the strings?... You don't. Well, that's great news, thank you, John. (*Then grimly*) Oh, listen, I may have to call you back. A little something has gone wrong at this end ... Yes. O.K. Thank you. (*He hangs up and starts across to Baldo menacingly*)

Alison (*anxiously, trying to stop him*) Now, wait, Sandy, we have all the papers ...

Sandy (*pushing her out of the way*) Yes, we have all the papers. (*He arrives to face Baldo blackly*) And you, you son-of-a-bitch, have lost the bodies.

Baldo eagerly takes hold of him and strokes his arm reassuringly

Baldo Not lost, Sandy, not lost. Maybe misplaced. How far can two bodies go in Rome?

Sandy (*angrily*) What the hell d'you mean, misplaced? Come on! !

Alison Sandy . . .

Baldo (*clinging to Sandy, pawing him*) No, listen, I went to the morgue, the public mortuary, La Casa Mortuaria . . .

Sandy (*overlapping, shoving him off*) Don't tell it from the beginning! What's happened to the bodies?

Alison Let him explain!

Sandy (*violently*) All right! Let him explain. (*To Baldo*) Go on!

Baldo Yes, I will tell you; I have a theory, I have a theory. You do not pay rent for the bodies at the public mortuary, e vero? Ah-ha! So! Maybe there is a government official who has a cousin who owns a private mortuary, and he has said, "We will move the bodies from the public mortuary to our own mortuary, and charge the rich American rent".

Sandy That's an explanation?

Baldo It's the best I can do.

Sandy Maybe that cousin who owns a private mortuary is a friend of yours, or an uncle! Where the hell is my father?

Baldo (*embracing and pawing him*) No, listen, Sandy, it is all right, we will find him . . .

Sandy (*pushing him off*) Keep your hands off me! (*He circles angrily around the armchair and back*)

Alison Sandy!

Sandy (*going right on*) God damn Italy and all Italians, why I ever hired a crook, a pimp and a hustler . . .

Alison Stop that! Stop it!

Baldo keeps following Sandy, anxiously pawing him like a puppy wanting to be loved

Baldo No, Alison, it is all right. Sandy, believe me, I will take care of everything—

Sandy
Baldo ⎰ Nobody knows how to do anything, everyone passes the buck, everyone gives you the run-around, everybody has his hand out . . . —and everything will be O.K. again. It will be like it was, and we will be happy, yes, happy . . . ⎱ (*Speaking together*)

Sandy brushes Baldo's embracing hands aside, grabs hold of him, and starts half pushing, half throwing him towards the stairs

Sandy Keep your hands off me and get out! Get out! Get out!

He flings Baldo away, and Baldo falls part way up the L stairs

Alison Ah, no!

Baldo scrambles to his feet and runs up on to the landing

   Baldo!

Baldo puts out a hand reassuringly

Baldo I'm all right.

Baldo looks at Sandy with a flash of entreaty, gets no answer, turns and runs out, leaving the door open

Alison (*blazing*) Who the bloody hell do you think you are? (*She grabs her hat and bag and races up the R steps*)
Sandy Alison, wait.

She stops on the landing, and looks down at him with fierce anger

Alison You great American tycoon! Why didn't you stay on your side of the ocean?! (*She turns and races out, calling*) Baldo!

Alison exits

Sandy ducks his head in despair, and moves down L, stunned by the sudden course of events. He sits on the armchair stool, lost for a moment. Then he suddenly gathers himself, rises quickly, and runs up the stairs

Sandy Alison!

Sandy races out of the room

The Lights fade to Black-out. The CURTAIN *remains up*

SCENE 2

The same. Later that afternoon

After a pause in the darkness, the Lights begin to come up slowly. The entrance doors to the room are closed. The Waiter is at the terrace doors, closing the shutters against the afternoon sun. He turns and starts across the room. He notices the empty glass that Baldo has left behind, picks it up, and moves to the drinks table. He puts the glass on his tray, on which is an empty San Pellegrino bottle. He inspects the drinks table, then, with the tray, turns to leave. The doors open, and Alison appears on the landing, looking forlorn. She closes the doors and starts down the L stairs. The Waiter moves up a little towards the fountain and greets her with a beaming smile

Waiter Ah, Signora Claiborne! I bring for you water and ice. (*He pronounces precisely*) Ice—ghiaccio. Capisce? (*He is pleased to be giving her another Italian lesson*) Ice! Ghiaccio!
Alison (*expressionless*) Thank you. (*She wanders into the room down L*)

The Waiter understands that she is not in the mood. He starts for the R stairs

Waiter Prego.

Alison looks at the open bedroom door. The Waiter sees this, and stops and tries again

Il Signore Claiborne is not in. Is out. You wish for something? (*No answer*) Signora Claiborne?
Alison (*gently*) Please don't call me that.
Waiter (*embarrassed*) Ah. Scusi.

The Waiter goes up the R stairs. Alison turns quickly

Alison Giorgio!

He pauses on the landing

I'm sorry.
Waiter (*with a loving, forgiving smile*) Niente. Niente.

The Waiter goes out

A moment. Alison looks about. She moves to the radio switch and turns it on. The voice of the Italian tenor singing "Arrivederci Roma" fills the room. Alison turns and wanders across the room. She puts her hat and bag on the desk, pushes open the shutter doors, and wanders out on to the terrace

After a moment the front doors open again and Sandy appears, looking tired and forlorn

He comes down into the room, looks about, does not know what to do. The sound of the singing bothers him, he goes and turns off the radio. He starts to move back into the room, then is arrested by the thought that someone must have turned the radio on. He looks about with quick hope, and calls

Sandy Alison?

Sandy runs into the bedroom

(*as he goes*) Alison!

After a moment, Alison wanders on from the terrace

Sandy dashes into the room, calling

Alison! (*He sees her, and stops short*) Ah, Alison. I'm so sorry. I'm so desperately, desperately sorry. (*No answer. He moves closer, below the sofa*) I've looked all over Rome for you. Up the Campidoglio, all through the Borghese Gardens. I even went to the Sistine Chapel.

And suddenly her face contorts with tears, and she races to him, and goes into his arms. He kisses her. She gently breaks away from him and moves down towards the desk

Alison That doesn't prove anything.
Sandy It helps. Did you find Baldo?

She shakes her head, and sits on the desk stool

The poor bastard. Where did you go?
Alison To the Spanish Steps.

Sandy Ah, I should have known. (*Tenderly*) You didn't buy any flowers.

Alison I didn't feel like it.

Sandy Ah, Alison, I'm so sorry.

Alison (*suddenly fiercely pleading*) But you're not the kind that beats people, I know you're not!

Sandy I don't want to be.

Alison Then don't be! Ah, Sandy—such an impatient young man. You have to have what you want when you want it.

Sandy I want you.

Alison I'm not sure, now.

Sandy I do.

Alison You won't, when we're apart.

Sandy I will.

Alison I may not want you.

Sandy I'd die if you didn't. Thank you for coming back.

Alison I had to come back. My clothes are scattered all over your room. And my suitcase is under the bed. (*She rises and goes towards the bedroom*)

Sandy You're not going.

Alison (*nodding*) Time to pack and get out.

Sandy Why?

Alison Because I'm such a disorderly person. And you hate disorder.

Sandy Not your kind.

Alison Only the Italian? Sandy, they do have fun.

Sandy Not because they're disorderly.

Alison Yes, exactly because they're disorderly, don't you see? (*She turns to the bedroom door*)

Sandy Don't pack. Please.

Alison I must.

The front door bangs open, and Baldo appears on the landing, as bright and cheerful as ever we saw him

Baldo (*crowing jubilantly*) BAL—DO! ! ! ! !

Sandy Baldo!

Alison Baldo!

They race to him, and he storms down the stairs and lifts Alison high in the air

Baldo Ho-ho! !

Alison (*from up in the air*) Baldassare Pantaleone!

Sandy Baldo, where have you been? Are you all right?

Baldo I am wonderful! (*He lowers Alison happily*)

Sandy (*in a hurry*) Baldo, I'm sorry, I apologize, that was the most terrible thing I've done in my life. I just don't know how to tell you . . .

Baldo (*overlapping him*) No, you must not, that is gone, finito! We are Baldo-Sandy even when we quarrel! (*He links arms with them and marches them down* L)

Sandy That's right.

Alison (*lovingly*) Ah, Baldo!

Baldo, between them, holds up his hands for attention

Baldo (*importantly*) Momento! (*He strikes a great pose*) I have found
them! Yes!

Alison Mother and father?

Baldo Yes!

Sandy Where?

Baldo (*jubilantly*) You see? I knew! It was exactly like I told you!

Sandy Where are they?

Baldo In a funeral parlour in the Parioli district. Not the best, but not
too bad. They are fine, they are happy, they look wonderful. Here is the
card. (*He hands Sandy a card, which is edged in black*) And ho-ho-ho!
Have I scared him!

Sandy Who?

Baldo (*pointing to the card*) This one who owns the funeral parlour. I was
right: he has a nephew who is a small something in the government. (*He
makes a rude noise*)

Sandy (*happily relieved*) It's O.K., I'll pay him, I don't care.

Baldo No, you will not! (*He laughs gleefully*) Madonna mia, he is so
scared!

Alison Why?

Baldo (*hooting with laughter*) Because I have told him that Sandy is the
beloved nephew of the President of the United States, and that they
have telephoned from Washington, and the Foreign Minister himself is
looking for the bodies. Ho! He did not know what to do first: to go to
confession, or go see his lawyer.

Sandy Baldo, you're marvellous!

*Without thinking, Sandy happily puts an arm around Baldo and gives him a
quick hug, and Baldo puts an arm around him*

And I'll pay him, just for the hell of it.

Baldo Well, a few thousand lire for the courtesy, hmmm? It is O.K., now,
hey? Everything is O.K.?

Sandy (*joyfully*) O.K.!

Baldo And I am marvellous? We are Baldo and Sandy again?

Sandy Yep.

They still have their arms round each other

Baldo (*impishly*) O.K.! Kiss me!

Alison laughs aloud. Sandy breaks away from Baldo quickly, but amused

(*Sympathetically*) You suffer so from morality.

Alison (*laughing*) Ah, Baldo, I'll kiss you. Although it won't be the same.
(*And she embraces him and kisses him on the cheek*)

Baldo Thank you. (*He looks reproachfully at Sandy*)

Sandy It isn't anything personal.

Baldo I can wait. (*He goes to the desk*) Ah, but now! Alison! The real
news! (*He sees his sunglasses*) My shades! (*He picks them up and puts
them on*) I have wonderful news for you. (*He picks up the phone*)

Alison (*following him*) What?

Baldo Magnifico! Wait! You will see! (*Into the phone*) Il bar, per favore. (*To Alison*) I will tell him you are here; he will come up.
Alison Who?

Sandy goes to stand with her

Baldo (*into the phone*) Bar? . . . Per piacere, il Signore Vittorio Spina. (*To Alison*) You have heard of Vittorio Spina, the great film director?
Alison No.
Baldo But he is one of the greatest film directors in the world! He has won an Oscar for Gina Lollobrigida, he has won an Oscar for Anna Magnani, he has won an Oscar for Marcello Mastroianni . . .
Sandy Has he won an Oscar for himself?

Baldo gestures as though to say a big " Yes", but the truth comes out

Baldo No. But this is politics. (*Into the phone*) Vittorio? . . . Baldo! (*Indicating Alison*) Sta cui! . . . Si! . . . (*Adoring her*) Ah, si, bellissima! Venite subito? . . . Va bene. (*He hangs up*) He comes!
Alison But why?
Baldo (*moving to the centre of the room; importantly*) Because! Alison! He is going to make a film in Spain, and he wants *you*!
Alison Me?! Where'd he ever hear of me?
Baldo From me! I met him in the lobby of the hotel, and he said, "Baldo, I need someone who speaks Spanish . . ."
Alison (*anxiously*) I don't speak Spanish.
Baldo I speak Spanish. You have to speak English!
Alison (*laughing breathlessly*) Oh, yes. I can manage that. (*It is the actress on the scent of a job*)
Baldo And so, I shall be his assistant. Assistant director, assistant producer, assistant writer, and also assistant to keep happy the two American stars, who hate each other. We go to Madrid on Friday.
Alison *This* Friday?!
Baldo Yes!
Alison But, Baldo, how can he engage me when he doesn't know what I can do?
Baldo I have told him! I have made a picture of you: the look, the tall, the eyes, the hair, the . . . (*He indicates her breasts*)
Alison (*hastily*) Yes, I know.
Baldo And I have told him of the great films you have made in London, and also the television commercial . . .
Alison Not that!
Baldo Ecco! I have done it for him! (*He raises his hands over his head in the ballet dancer's position and imitates Alison's TV commercial dance, dancing towards them so that they have to break* R) "Tinkle, tinkle, tinkle —phoom!" (*He drops to his knees and spreads his arms*)
Alison (*aghast*) You mean you gave that imitation of me, and he wants me?
Baldo (*proudly*) Ecco! He says you are a great tragedienne. Ah, and Alison, Madrid! You have never been to Spain?
Alison No.

Baldo (*taking her hands and whirling her to the centre of the room*) Ho! It
is really something!

There is a knock at the door

Porter (*off*) Permesso?

Baldo (*in a nervous panic*) He comes! (*Calling*) Momento! (*He pulls
Alison to the stool* L, *seats her, arranges her, crosses her legs, pushes her
skirt up, examines her*)

Alison (*pushing her skirt down*) What's he like?

Baldo (*pushing her skirt up*) Charming!

Alison pushes her skirt down

Porter (*off*) Permesso!

Baldo Avanti!

He rushes up towards the L *stairs, then looks back at Alison. She promptly
pulls her skirt part of the way up*

> *The Porter pushes both doors open and steps back. Vittorio Spina sweeps
> in. The Porter closes the door, disappearing. Spina strikes a pose on the
> landing. Baldo was right: he is a charmer, and knows it. He is in his fifties,
> short and stocky. His dark hair is greying handsomely, and he has a fine,
> dark moustache. He shows his teeth a lot: he has a bright, flashing smile
> that makes him seem all beautiful white teeth. He wears a soft, black,
> rather wide-brimmed hat at a rather rakish angle. The dark topcoat is
> flung over his shoulders like a cape. Beneath it is a dark grey striped suit.
> His feet are beautifully shod. His pose on the landing is perfect*

Spina starts down the R *stairs as Baldo rushes to the foot of them, effectively
screening Alison from Spina's view as he introduces Sandy, who is above the
desk*

  Vittorio! Entri! Caro! Le presento il famoso ingengnere Americano,
  Alexander Ben Claiborne!

Spina (*loftily, as he comes down*) Adoro l'America e tutti gli Americani.
(*He takes Sandy's hand*) Piacere.

Sandy Hello.

Baldo takes Spina's hat and coat, and makes a grand gesture

Baldo Eccola! La vedetta Inglese! Alison Ames!

*Spina turns and looks across the room to Alison, and almost swoons. Baldo
drops the hat and coat on the sofa*

Spina Alison ! ! ! ! Ames ! ! ! ! (*He goes to her imperiously, and kisses
her hand*)

Alison (*in her best graceful manner*) How do you do?

Baldo comes down L *to hover near them anxiously. Spina keeps Alison's
hand and raises her, then leads her out into the room. He moves around her,
examining her as though she were a great work of art. As he gets behind her,
he quite obviously puts his hand on her bottom, for she suddenly gives a small,*

startled, forward thrust of her pelvic region. But she keeps her cool. Sandy's eyes narrow, and he moves down to the desk. Spina moves to Baldo and smiles approvingly and makes a small gesture with his hand

Spina Belleza. Piccolino.
Baldo He likes you.
Alison (*not moving*) I could tell.

Now Spina raises his hands and interlocks them to make a viewer, and starts to move round her again, inspecting her as though through a camera. He comes to a stop R of her

Spina Bellissima.
Alison Prego.
Spina Ah! Parla Italiano!
Alison (*primly*) Divieto di sosta.

Spina laughs as though it were the greatest joke in the world, and moves past her again, towards Baldo. In passing, he gives her bottom another caress, and once again she gives that sudden forward thrust

Sandy (*moving towards Spina*) Hey, come on!
Alison (*quickly*) I'm all right, darling!
Baldo (*anxiously*) No, Sandy, please!

Sandy moves to Spina, who sits down promptly on the stool near the armchair and leans back apprehensively, wondering what this American is going to do next. Sandy stares down at him

Sandy (*with cool authority*) What's he going to give her besides his hand?
Spina (*smiling up at him hopefully*) Come?
Sandy (*all business*) Come on, Baldo, what's he going to pay her?

Sandy and Spina stare at each other

Baldo (*to Spina*) Vorebbe sapere quanto lei paga.
Spina Ah! (*He smiles up at Sandy with magnificent generosity*) Cinquanta mille.
Baldo Fifty thousand lire a week.

Alison, amazed and triumphant, dashes to stand at Sandy's back

Alison Fifty thousand lire a week!
Sandy (*over his shoulder*) About thirty pounds.
Alison Oh! (*She looks at Spina reproachfully*)
Spina (*with a happy smile*) Va bene?
Sandy (*imperturbably*) Tell him she's got to have seventy-five thousand a week and expenses.
Baldo (*shocked*) Sandy!
Alison Don't muck this up!
Sandy (*smiling down at Spina*) Tell him.
Spina (*smiling back at Sandy*) Che dice?
Baldo Desidera settenta cinque mille con spesi personali.

The smile disappears from Spina's face

Spina (*imperially*) Fuori discussione! (*He rises in his indignation and stalks to the centre of the room*)
Baldo (*following him*) Out of the question.
Sandy O.K., the deal's off.
Alison (*grabbing Sandy*) Now, wait a minute!
Sandy I know what I'm doing. Harvard Business School. Back me up.
Alison (*magnificently imperious*) Fuori discussione! ! ! !
Sandy At-a-girl!

Spina looks across at them, and has an idea. He speaks to Baldo

Spina Digli che e una parte meravigliosa. Diglielo!
Sandy What?
Baldo He says it is a marvellous part.

Spina goes to Alison, takes her by the hand, and leads her towards the centre of the room

Spina Digli che e una ragazza Inglese di tanti secoli fa——
Baldo She plays the part of an English girl of many centures ago——

Sandy sits in the armchair L. *Spina walks round Alison*

Spina —che e statta fatta prigionera dai Romani——
Baldo (*moving towards Sandy*) —who has been captured by the Romans—
Spina (*taking Alison in his arms intensely*) —ed e diventata l'amante del Generale Romano!
Baldo —and has become the mistress of the Roman General!

Spina bends Alison backwards in an embrace that would have done credit to Rudolph Valentino, and makes violent love to her with sudden fury, kissing her rapidly on the neck and shoulders. Then, just as suddenly, he straightens her up and walks away

Alison Wow.
Spina (*moving back to the centre of the room*) Dumque. Lui l'apporta in Ispagne col suo esercito——
Baldo Now he has brought you to Spain with his army——
Spina (*dramatically*) Perche?
Baldo (*moving to Spina*) Why?
Spina Perche!
Baldo Because!
Spina Deve impedire ad Alessandro Magno di conquistare il mondo!
Baldo He has to stop Alexander the Great from conquering the world!
Spina Dumque. In principio, lei detesta quel Generale Romano.
Baldo At first you hate this Roman General.
Spina (*with emotion*) Ma poi lui e fatto prigionero d' Alessandro Magno——
Baldo But then he is made prisoner of Alexander the Great——
Spina —e lei accorge di amarlo!
Baldo —and you realize that you love him!
Spina (*his eyes gleaming, for now comes the best part of the story*) E poi!
Baldo And then!
Spina E poi!

Baldo And then!
Alison (*in a small enquiring voice*) E poi?

Spina looks at her, startled, then goes back into his story dramatically. And Baldo, caught up in the drama of it, acts it out with him, every move

Spina E poi! Cosi! Di notte! (*He crouches down and begins to creep, stealthily*)
Baldo (*imitating him*) And so! At night!
Spina Gatton gattoni——
Baldo Like a cat——

Spina stalks stealthily, bent over in cat-like motions, around Sandy's chair. Baldo follows in exact imitation

Spina —riesce a penetrare nell'esercito nemico——
Baldo —you creep through the enemy lines——
Spina (*rising to his full height*) —va fino al padiglione di Alessandro Magno—— (*He pushes back the imaginary tent flap*)
Baldo (*doing the same*) —and you enter the tent of Alexander the Great——
Spina (*climactically, moving to Alison*) —ed offre il suo bel corpo per la vita del suo amante! ! (*And in front of Alison he makes the grand gesture of opening his jacket wide to offer his fair white body*)
Baldo (*following suit*) —and you offer your fair white body for the life of your lover!

The two men are posed before Alison

Alison (*looking over at Sandy*) Hey, that's not bad.
Spina (*overcome with his acting*) You like? (*To Sandy*) You like?
Sandy (*calmly*) Seventy-five thousand and expenses.
Baldo (*to Spina*) Settanta cinque mille con spesi.
Spina Settanta mille con spesi!
Baldo (*to Sandy*) Seventy thousand and expenses.
Sandy (*rising*) Seventy-three.
Baldo Settanta tre!
Spina Settanta uno!
Baldo Seventy-one!
Sandy Seventy-two!
Baldo Settanta due!
Spina Fatto!
Baldo Done!
Sandy Sold!

Spina and Baldo shake hands and embrace. Sandy crosses the room swiftly to Alison and embraces her, and they are both laughing

Alison How did you do it?!
Sandy You have to take your chances.

Spina happily goes to Alison, takes her by the hand, and leads her to the centre of the room. He drops his hand towards her bottom

Spina My star!

Alison deftly does a curtsy that drops her away from his hand, leaving it in view

Alison My director!

Spina laughs admiringly, and turns to Sandy to shake hands. Baldo picks up his coat and hat

Spina (*to Sandy*) Molto piacere.
Sandy Grazie.

Spina shakes a finger at him.

Spina Verrrrrrry smart! (*He turns to start out*)

Baldo drapes Spina's coat over his shoulders, and gives him his hat

    Vado da basso. Nel Bar.
Baldo Va bene. (*To the others*) He will wait in the bar.
Spina (*going up the* R *stairs*) Andiamo a Passetto, eh? Pranzare.
Baldo He wants us to have dinner with him.

Sandy looks hesitant, wondering if that includes him. Spina sees this

Spina Ma tutti!
Baldo (*to Sandy*) You, too.

Sandy looks at Alison. She nods

Sandy We accept.
Baldo (*to Spina*) Grazie. A piu tardi, Vittorio.

Spina, on the landing, puts on his hat, strikes a pose, and makes a loving gesture to Alison

Spina Alison! Ames!

And then Spina makes the Italian gesture of farewell, turns, and is gone, leaving the door open behind him

Baldo races up the stairs and closes the doors, then races down again gleefully

Alison I got the job!
Baldo (*going to her*) Ho-ho! ! ! !
Alison (*rubbing her behind*) I had a feeling I was going to get it. (*She runs across to Sandy*) Darling, you were absolutely marvellous! You'd make a wonderful white slaver. What's seventy-two thousand lire?
Sandy About forty-three pounds.
Alison I think I'll keep calling it seventy-two thousand lire. (*She dashes back to Baldo*) We're going to Spain! We're going to make a movie in Spain!

Alison and Baldo do a little Spanish victory dance, and sing

Alison { We're going to Spain— }
Baldo { We're going to Spain } (*Singing together*)

Baldo simulates the brandishing of a torero's muleta, and Alison puts her fingers to her head as horns and becomes a bull, then charges at Baldo

Baldo Toro! Toro! Hunh! Hunh!

Alison charges past him, he makes a graceful turn, she turns and charges past him again and runs right into Sandy's arms. He holds her close, lovingly. Pause

Sandy (*gently*) What will you do about your mother?

Alison looks at him and smiles

Alison Ah, well, yes, that's all right. I'd already decided about that. Before this happened. Sitting on the Spanish Steps, I decided I wanted to bury her here, where she died, because she loved it so, here. And there's nothing in England to call her back, really. No family but me. And I'd rather come back to see her here. It is possible, Baldo, isn't it?

Baldo Certo.

Alison I think there's an English graveyard here in Rome . . .

Baldo Yes. It is where your poets, Shelley and Keats, are buried.

Alison Ah, that! She'd like that. (*She smiles up at Sandy*)

Sandy (*after a moment*) Would there be room for my father?

Alison What?

The sun is beginning to set. Dusk has begun to enter the room

Sandy Baldo, will they take an American in that English graveyard?

Baldo Oh, I do not think the dead are anti-American. (*He sits on the stool near the armchair*)

Alison What are you talking about?

Sandy (*in a matter-of-fact tone*) I'm going with you.

Alison Where?

Sandy Spain, London, wherever you go. I'm going with you.

Alison (*anxiously*) No, I don't know what you mean.

Sandy (*exuberantly, almost shouting it*) I'm going with you! For ever!

Alison (*staring at Sandy*) You're out of your mind.

Sandy I'm blowing my mind. I'm blowing my world.

Alison You can't.

Sandy Why? Because I'm married and have children and a Lincoln Continental?

Alison Yes. And the world that goes with it. It's not that easy to walk out on your world. You said it yourself.

Sandy (*joyously*) I didn't know what I was missing, then.

Alison You're being a romantic ass. The world well lost for love! That's gone out.

Sandy (*joyously*) Never! Never! And if you think I'm going to let you go off with that old lecher . . .

Alison I don't have to sleep with him for forty-three pounds a week.

Sandy Don't think he hasn't got it in mind.

Alison Baldo will be there!

Sandy To protect you? He'd be in there with you!

And then he waves an apology to Baldo, who waves back forgiveness

Alison Is that why you want to come along? To protect me?

Sandy Yes! No! I want to be with you, don't you understand? I want to be with you! For always. (*Gently*) Don't you want me?

Alison (*gently*) I don't want to ruin your life.

Sandy (*loving her for saying it*) How could you ruin my life? I can work anywhere, I'm a good business man. There isn't anything I can't do if I put my hand to it. Let me come with you.

A moment

Baldo (*genuinely moved*) You would do this for her truly? Leave everything behind to go away with her?

Sandy nods. Alison pulls back from him a bit to look up at him

Alison (*softly*) Forsaking all others?

Sandy nods

You wouldn't fool a girl?

Sandy shakes his head

What of your father?

Sandy Let him lie next to your mother, where he would want to be, in a graveyard in Rome where Keats and Shelley are buried.

Alison Can you do that?

Sandy I can make a large try. (*A moment*) Yes?

Alison Yes.

Baldo (*rising exuberantly*) Oho! Celebration! Lights! (*He races up to the landing to turn on the lights*)

Sandy Lights!

Alison All the lights!

They dash about turning on the lights

Baldo (*racing down the stairs again*) It is like New Year's Eve! We should blow trumpets!

Sandy Beat drums!

Alison Throw confetti!

Baldo In Italy, we throw things out the window! Old dishes, old brooms, old pots and pans . . .

Alison What if someone gets hit?

Baldo Peccato! Too bad!

Sandy Peccato!

Alison Peccato!

Baldo And then on New Year's Day, we buy everything new . . .

Sandy Everything new tomorrow! What'll we throw?

Alison Old flowers!

Sandy Old flowers!

Alison New ones tomorrow!

They all three snatch up vases of flowers. Baldo has the vase that contains only daffodils. They circle the room in file, Alison in the lead, then Baldo, then Sandy, and head towards the terrace, singing

Alison ⎡ "We three Kings of Orient are!   ⎤
Baldo ⎨ Bearing gifts, we travel afar!   ⎬ *(Singing*
Sandy ⎣ Field and fountain, moor and mountain . . ." ⎦ *together)*

Halfway through their singing, the front doors open and the Porter appears, carrying Diana's suitcase

Their singing fades away as they see him, and they stop near the terrace doors

Porter (*as he crosses into the bedroom*) Buona sera.
Baldo (*mechanically*) Buona sera.

The Porter exits to the bedroom. We hear voices in the corridor, and the Assistant Manager comes backing in, followed by Diana, who is in another smart travelling costume. The Assistant Manager is distraught

Assistant Manager (*as he enters*) I am so sorry, Mrs Claiborne, but nobody told us you were coming, nobody, I assure you.
Diana (*firmly, abruptly*) O.K.! O.K.!

Sandy moves to the foot of the R stairs. The Assistant Manager is directly above him, Diana L on the landing

Assistant Manager But I am delighted that you have come back to us! (*He looks at Sandy grimly, takes one step down, and reaches out*) Mr Claiborne, here is a cable for you!

Sandy takes the cable. The Assistant Manager draws himself up

The hotel assumes no responsibility!

The Assistant Manager turns and marches out swiftly

Diana starts down the L stairs

Sandy Where'd you come from?
Diana The airport. Why didn't you meet me?
Sandy I didn't know you were coming.
Diana I sent you a cable.
Sandy The only cable I got said, "Congratulations, you're a grandfather".
Diana That's not the cable I sent. What does that say?

Sandy puts his vase of flowers down on the table behind the sofa, and opens the telegram

Sandy It says you're coming.
Diana I'm here.

Sandy moves to her and they embrace briefly. She moves below the sofa

Who are your friends?
Sandy Baldo Pantaleone, Alison Ames, my wife Diana.
Diana How do you do?

Alison (*quietly*) How do you do? (*She moves down to the desk, puts her vase of flowers down, and remains there*)

Baldo (*moving to Diana cheerfully*) Welcome to Rome, Signora Claiborne! I am the one you talked to on the telephone.

Diana (*coolly*) Oh, yes, the man who's supposed to fix everything.

Baldo (*nicely*) I do my best. (*He pulls a daffodil from the vase he holds, and hands it to her*) Complimenti.

Diana (*taking it*) Thank you. I've heard a lot about you.

Baldo In America?

Diana Yes.

Baldo (*pleased*) From who, please?

The Porter comes out of the bedroom and starts for the stairs. Diana turns

Diana Take care of him, Sandy.

Sandy tips the Porter

The Porter goes out

Baldo goes above the sofa and puts his vase on the table

Where'd all the flowers come from?

Sandy (*curtly*) Baldo bought them.

Baldo I admire flowers.

Diana Why were you dancing round the room with them?

Sandy It's an old Roman custom.

Baldo Yes, in Rome, when we celebrate, we throw flowers out the window.

Diana Vases and all? How ostentatious.

Baldo We like the noise.

Diana What were you celebrating?

Alison (*abruptly*) We're going to Spain.

Diana Who?

A moment. Alison finds she cannot do it

Alison Baldo and I.

Baldo (*moving quickly to Alison*) Si! We are going to Spain to make an Italian movie for the American market. With armies and elephants and cannons—also actors. And Alison Ames will be the star. She is a great actress. And beautiful, no? Com' e bella! (*He embraces Alison*)

Diana stares across at Alison, and her eyes narrow with sudden realization

Diana Alison Ames. I could kick myself. You're the one. (*She crosses the room and comes to a stop before Alison*)

Baldo puts out his hand protectively with a strangled outcry

Baldo We are going to be married.

Diana Complimenti. (*She puts the daffodil in Baldo's hand. She stares at Alison*) You're the one whose mother was killed in the accident.

Alison Oh. Yes.

Diana I should have realized. I'm terribly sorry.

Alison It's all right.

Diana What a wicked, wasteful thing that your mother, a total stranger . . .

Sandy (*behind Diana*) She wasn't a stranger!

Diana Well, naturally, they'd met. (*To Alison*) How did they meet, Miss Ames?

Sandy In Perugia!

Diana All right, Sandy. (*To Alison*) Just in passing, the way tourists do, I suppose.

Alison Yes.

Diana And he offered her a lift. Fate does play terrible tricks, doesn't it?

Alison Yes.

Sandy Diana, how did you know? That her mother was killed in the crash with father?

Diana From the State Department.

Sandy What State Department?

Diana How many State Departments are there?

Sandy Washington? You went to Washington?

Diana Yes. (*She moves to him proudly*)

Sandy (*devastated*) You went to Washington and threw your weight about and pulled strings and got all this done? From there?

Diana (*airily*) Yes. (*She sits on the sofa, terribly pleased with herself*)

Baldo (*with quiet despair*) Madonna mia.

Diana (*brightly*) Well, I decided if I was ever going to get my husband home, I'd better go into action.

Sandy (*in a dead tone*) What did you do, Diana?

Diana Oh, I called Connie Dudley and said, "Who do you know?", and it turned out she knew everybody. So, I flew to Washington, and went to the State Department——

Sandy (*hopelessly*) —and saw the Secretary of State . . .

Diana (*brightly*) Yes, he just happened to be in town. And he got right on the phone to Rome and raised hell. Then we had lunch with the Italian Ambassador, who patted me in all the right places, and he got on the phone to Rome and raised hell. (*To Alison*) There's something so normal about being pinched by an Italian, isn't there? (*Back to Sandy*) And there you are. Did you get my message from Washington?

Sandy Yes.

Diana It was really no effort. Oh, that's where I heard about you, Mr Pantaleone.

Baldo (*momentarily cheered*) From our Ambassador.

Diana (*coolly*) No, his chauffeur. (*She rises, with her handbag*) Now, if you'll excuse me, I think I'll retire to that great big beautiful bedroom. (*She heads for the bedroom*)

Alison gives a quick scream of horror

Alison Ah! ! !

Baldo (*covering her immediately*) Ah! ! !

Diana (*stopping short*) What's the matter?

Baldo goes swiftly and gets between Diana and the bedroom door

Baldo I am so sorry, but I suddenly remembered that in the bedroom are some clothes—of mine—and a suitcase.
Diana Oh?
Baldo (*at his most charming*) And I must get them out of your way, no? You see, my flat was being painted yesterday, and the smell of the paint . . . (*He feigns being terribly ill*) And so I asked Sandy if I could sleep here.

Diana looks from Baldo to Sandy with some amusement

Diana Well, that is a big bed, isn't it?
Baldo Oh, I slept on the floor. Permesso?

Baldo bows and goes into the bedroom, closing the door

Diana (*turning, amused*) And where did you sleep, Miss Ames?
Sandy (*angrily*) Diana!
Diana So sorry. (*She moves to Alison*) Are you really getting married?
Alison We've talked about it.
Diana Did you meet here in Rome?
Alison Yes.
Diana Well, Rome is the place, isn't it? (*She moves up to look out of the terrace windows with great pleasure*) What a view! The Pines of Rome! (*Over her shoulder, to Alison*) That's a famous piece of music, you know. By Respighi.
Sandy (*quietly depressed*) My wife is on the board of the St Louis Symphony.
Diana (*turning, cheerfully*) President of the Board! (*She goes to Sandy, dropping her bag on the sofa as she goes*) Darling, do you mind if we stay over until Thursday night? We don't have to be home until Friday.
Sandy Why? What's Friday?
Diana I've arranged a memorial service for your father, and right after that, a board of directors meeting.
Sandy What board of directors meeting?
Diana Yours.
Sandy What do you mean? What's happened?

Diana laughs happily, takes him by the arm and draws him away down L

Diana Well! You're going to like this. Excuse us, Miss Ames, family business. (*To Sandy, cosily*) I had a long talk with the company lawyers, and then I called in your mother and your sisters and Jack O'Connor, and it all went smooth as silk. They're going to give you voting control of their shares, you're going to have complete control of the company. How about that? There'll be a news release in the Sunday papers.
Sandy (*grimly*) The Sunday papers. And you did it.
Diana (*happily*) You're going to be able to do every damned thing you ever planned and dreamed of.
Sandy And you did it.
Diana (*modestly*) Oh, I was just there, that's all. If you'd been there in-

stead of here . . . So, do you mind if we stay until Thursday night?
There's one thing I am absolutely determined to do before I leave Rome.
I want to see the Sistine Chapel. (*She smiles over at Alison*) Have you
seen it, Miss Ames?

Alison (*flatly*) Yes. It's memorable.

Diana (*moving to her*) I adore Michelangelo.

*As Diana moves, the bedroom door opens and Baldo enters with Alison's
suitcase. But he has done a hasty job of packing, and lacy bits of feminine
apparel hang out at the ends.*

Sandy sees this, and points frantically

Sandy Baldo, why don't you put that down and stay awhile?! (*He pushes
Baldo behind the armchair*)

Baldo (*looking down*) Ah, yes, si! (*He ducks down behind the armchair and
repacks*)

Alison (*picking up her hat and bag*) I'm afraid we must be going.

Diana (*starting back above the sofa towards the bedroom*) No, don't go
because of me. I'm going to unpack and have a bath. I'm sure you and
Sandy still have things to talk about. I don't know what arrangements
were made about your mother. I was only concerned with his father.

Alison Yes, of course.

Baldo comes up from behind the armchair

Diana You know what's been bugging me ever since I left this place? That
damned fountain. If something's supposed to work, it ought to work.
(*She goes to the fountain and turns the knob. Nothing happens*) Work,
damn you! (*She stamps on the floor and turns away*)

The fountain lights up, and the water plays. Diana stops and turns

Ah!

Baldo (*moving up past Diana*) You should be Italian, Signora.

Diana I'm beginning to catch on. Good luck with your movie, Mr
Pantaleone. Good-bye, Miss Ames. Have fun in Spain.

Diana waves a hand and goes into the bedroom, closing the door

Pause. Sandy goes and turns off the fountain. Baldo puts down the suitcase

Baldo (*gently, sadly*) I have not taken the flowers out of the bathtub.

Sandy (*flatly*) She'll manage.

Baldo This, one can see.

Sandy I won't be going to Spain.

Alison This one can see, also.

Sandy (*turning on her fiercely*) It isn't that easy!

They stare at each other. Baldo picks up the suitcase and moves to the L
stairs. Sandy turns to him

I'll see you again.

Baldo I don't know. (*He starts up the stairs*)

Sandy Don't sell me short. I'll see you again.

Baldo (*from halfway up the stairs; sadly, wryly*) We play games. And then—suddenly—everything is real.

Sandy (*strongly*) I'll see you again.

Baldo Magari. I hope. (*He smiles nicely, and goes up the stairs. To Alison*) I will wait in the bar.

Sandy has thought of something. He draws from his inside pocket a flat pack of thousand-lire notes, and goes swiftly to the foot of the stairs

Sandy Baldo, wait, I haven't paid you.

Baldo (*violently*) No! No! No!

Sandy I've got to pay you.

Baldo No! No! No!

Sandy (*strongly, grimly*) Baldo, so help me, you're going to take it. One way or another, I'll get it to you. You're going to have it. (*Gently*) Please.

It is a deeply felt plea, a need for forgiveness and acceptance. And Baldo knows it. Sandy moves up one step, reaches out, and puts the money in Baldo's hand

Baldo Grazie. (*He puts the money in his pocket*)

For a moment the two men regard each other

Arrivederci.

Sandy Arrivederci.

Baldo goes out

Sandy looks over at Alison, and comes down to the centre of the room

What did you expect? Something mousey and mean?

Alison Yes! And horrible! I wanted her to be horrible! (*She is angry and resentful, and feels destroyed*)

Sandy Why would I marry anybody horrible?

Alison You didn't have to marry a star! She's a star!

Sandy I love you!

Alison Rubbish! ! ! ! I know what it's been, now. The short, lovely affair of Alison Ames—and the return of the Lincoln Continental. (*With her hat and her bag, she starts out*)

Sandy (*moving swiftly to her*) Look: you were right, I'm a romantic fool. I'm not going to run away with you. But that doesn't change anything!

Alison Oh, yes it does!

She tries to dodge around him to get to the front door. He catches hold of her and holds her tightly

Sandy I love you, I want you!

Alison (*breaking loose*) Let me go!

Sandy Alison, please!

They face each other, speaking with the low intensity of not wanting to be heard in the next room

Alison You can't want me!

Sandy I do!

Alison Then you're a bloody damned fool, because I'm not a star, never a star, and she is. (*She is close to angry tears*)

Sandy Maybe I don't want to live with a star.

Alison Ho-o-o-! ! !

Sandy (*overlapping*) I want you!

Alison As what? A concubine?

Sandy Alison, please believe me. Nothing has changed, everything I said was true. Give me a chance to work things out.

Alison (*gently, scanning his face lovingly*) But she owns you, don't you see? You belong to her.

Sandy I want to belong to you.

Alison For part of the time? Come on, be honest. You'd like what your father had, wouldn't you? One month a year.

Sandy I just don't want you to walk out of my life.

Alison What else can I do?

He stares at her, lost

> *The bedroom door opens, and Diana appears in the doorway wearing a lovely négligé*

Diana Sandy, dear. (*As she talks she moves to the sofa, gets her bag, and moves back to the bedroom door*) Oh, I'm sorry, Miss Ames. I thought you had gone. Darling, when you've finished, would you come and do something about all those flowers? I've got the ones out of the bathtub, but I do really feel as though I ought to be laid out.

Sandy (*tightly*) Yes.

Diana Your friend must be mad. Why would anyone buy so many flowers?

Sandy I don't know.

Diana Well, get someone to take them away, will you?

Sandy Yes.

Diana And do come in soon.

Diana starts to turn back to the bedroom, and at that moment there is a quick bang on the door, and we hear Wesley call

Wesley (*off; in a hurry*) Permesso avanti!

> *Wesley opens the door as he speaks, and bursts into the room, seeing only Sandy and Alison. He speaks quickly to Sandy*

Listen, I just heard at the Embassy that your wife . . . (*And he sees Diana*) Oh! You're here! ! ! (*He tries to look overjoyed, and, in his eagerness to cover up, makes a move towards her, forgetting that he is on the landing. He slips, slides and stumbles down the stairs, and lands on all fours. He looks across to Diana, smiling eagerly*) Welcome back!

Diana That is the warmest welcome I've ever had.

Wesley retrieves his glasses and rises to his feet, breathing hard, looking anxious, trying to look happy. Sandy moves behind the sofa

Wesley I just came over to see if—you were all right, and—if everything was—all right.

Diana Yes, thank you, everything's fine.

Wesley It is? Well, that's fine. (*He looks quickly at Sandy*)

Sandy Yes, everything's fine.

Wesley That's fine. (*With a sigh of relief*) Well!

Diana Is there something you wanted to say to me? Or my husband?

Wesley No—no—I just wanted to see if everything was all right, and— everything's fine, isn't it?

Diana Yes, fine. (*To Sandy*) How do we end this conversation?

Sandy (*gently*)) Why don't you go and take your bath, Diana?

Diana That's a *fine* idea. (*She extends her hand*) Good-bye, Mr Wesley. Will we see you at the airport?

Wesley (*shaking her hand firmly*) Sure! Fine!

Diana You win. (*She nods appealingly at Sandy, and turns to the bedroom door*) Sandy?

Diana goes into the bedroom, closing the door

Wesley looks at Sandy and Alison apologetically

Wesley Gee, I almost blew it, didn't I? I'm sorry.

Sandy (*grimly, turning up to the windows*) No, you didn't, John.

Alison It was sweet of you to try to warn us.

Wesley (*anxiously*) What are you two going to do?

Alison About what?

Wesley (*coming closer to her*) Listen, I've been around you two all week, and I know it wasn't just an ordinary shack-up. I guess this is the end, huh?

Sandy (*lost*) I guess.

Alison (*smiling at the inevitable*) Oh—I think you'll see us again, John.

Wesley I will?

Sandy whirls, not sure he heard right

Sandy You mean that?

Alison nods. Sandy goes quickly down and faces across to her

You'll do it!

Alison Yes!

Sandy You will!

She nods happily, emotionally

You really will!

She keeps nodding, quickly, almost laughing. Wesley hovers behind her

Wesley She will what?

Sandy (*intently, stepping closer to her*) One month a year!

Alison For starters! !

Sandy For starters! ! (*He raises his arms and gives the most expressive silent whoop of happiness ever seen or heard in this world*)

Alison (*joyously*) Wouldn't Mother laugh!
Sandy And Father!

They fall into each other's arms in a great embrace, and kiss

Wesley (*hovering*) Laugh at what? Hey, fellas . . .

Sandy and Alison break apart

Alison (*with a laughing, heartfelt cry*) Ah, but Sandy, I don't think I can wait until next May!
Sandy October!
Alison Can you manage it?
Sandy Yes!

They are speaking in breathless haste

Alison D'you think you can?
Sandy Yes!
Alison Where will we meet? Perugia?
Sandy Here! Right here!
Alison The royal suite!
Sandy Yes!

Wesley finally understands, and is delighted

Wesley Oh! Hey! That's great!

Sandy and Alison do not know he is there

Alison The first of October!
Sandy Yes!
Alison Will we have a month?
Sandy Yes!
Alison You promise! A full month!
Sandy I promise! I promise!
Wesley That's just great!

Alison laughs, her head high, and suddenly she seems a foot taller, and proud possessor of all she surveys. There is a new radiance. She puts her straw hat on the back of her head and smiles at the two men with queenly grace, then takes a long sigh

Alison (*the actress, the star*) And now—now that I am to be a star—I should like to go—attended. Would you escort me, John, to the bar downstairs, where my assistant, Baldassare Pantaleone, waits? With my director?
Wesley I would be honoured.
Alison (*with grace*) For, you see, I'm to be the star of a film made in Spain.
Wesley You are?
Sandy (*adoringly*) Yes, she is.

Alison looks at Sandy, and smiles

Alison Until October . . .

Sandy nods. She takes Wesley's arm, and they turn and move to the L stairs, and start up. Halfway up, Alison stops and turns, and Wesley continues up to the landing to wait. Alison looks across to Sandy and smiles

   Ciao . . .

Sandy (*raising his hand*) Ciao . . .

Alison has a sudden moment of fright, remembering what Baldo said: "And we may never see him again", but she recovers at once, and smiles across at Sandy

Alison (*lovingly*) Ciao . . .

Alison turns and starts up the stairs again, as—

the CURTAIN *falls*

FURNITURE AND PROPERTY LIST

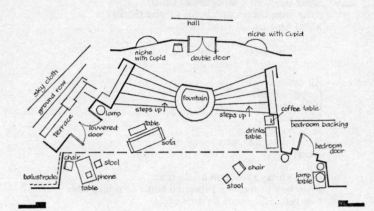

ACT I

SCENE 1

On stage: Small coffee table

Drinks table. *On it:* Carpano bottle, 2 serviettes, Jack Daniels bottle, Pellegrino bottle, 5 whisky glasses, 2 aperitif glasses, 2 wine glasses, ashtray, empty ice bucket

Armchair with stool below it. *On chair:* cushion

Sofa. *On it:* 2 cushions

Sofa table. *On it:* travelling bag with 2 magazines

Desk. *On it:* lamp, desk pad with paper and envelopes, ink stand, 2 ball-point pens, telephone, telephone directory, buzzer, 3 American Express labels, 3 unopened letters. *Beside it:* wastepaper basket

Desk stool

Console table. *On it:* ashtray, lamp

2 small chairs

Fountain

2 Cupids in niches

On walls: radio speaker and switch, mirror

Off stage: Handbag and over-shoulder bag **(Diana)**

2 suitcases **(Sandy)**

Briefcase with 2 official forms **(Wesley)**

Silver tray with 3 small cups and saucers, 3 spoons, sugar bowl, coffee pot, pad, pencil **(Waiter)**

Personal: **Sandy:** bandage, roll of lire notes, watch
              Baldo: notebook, ball-point pen, watch, comb, sunglasses
              Alison: handbag with comb, lipstick, compact, handkerchief

SCENE 2

Set: Window shutters closed

Off stage: Silver tray with 3 wineglasses **(Alison)**
              Silver wine bucket with bottle of wine **(Sandy)**
              Metal wine bucket stand **(Baldo)**

ACT II
SCENE 1

Strike: All dirty glasses
              Carpano bottle
              Pellegrino bottle
              Silver tray
              Wine bucket stand
              Wine bucket and wine
              Jacket

Set: Clean whisky glasses on drinks table
              Silver tray with empty Pellegrino bottle on drinks table
              Full Pellegrino bottle on drinks table
              Ice bucket on drinks table
              Wesley's briefcase and hat on sofa
              Flowers as follows:
                  Vase of daffodils on coffee table
                  Vase of roses on desk
                  Single rose on desk pad
                  Vase of lilac and peonies on console table
                  Pot of lilacs, etc. by standard lamp
                  Urn of mixed flowers down R
                  Roses, daffodils, narcissus around cupids
              Window shutters and bedroom door open
              Double doors closed

Off stage: Large bunch of flowers **(Alison)**
              Package of lire notes **(Sandy)**

Personal: **Alison:** cable
              Sandy: Lire notes
              Baldo: sunglasses

SCENE 2

Set: Main doors closed

Off stage: Funeral card **(Baldo)**
              2 suitcases **(Porter)**
              Cable **(Assistant Manager)**
              Alison's suitcase with lacy clothing hanging out **(Baldo)**

Personal: **Sandy:** wad of lire notes

LIGHTING PLOT

Property fittings required: chandelier, wall brackets, desk lamp, standard lamp, table lamp, fountain light

Interior. A hotel apartment. The same scene throughout

ACT I, SCENE 1. Day

To open: General effect of warm spring sunshine

Cue 1	**Baldo:** "Movite!" *Fountain lights up and plays*	(Page 24)
Cue 2	**Baldo** exits *Fade to Black-out*	(Page 24)

ACT I, SCENE 2. Night

To open: Darkness

Cue 3	At start of Scene *Fade up to moonlight effect*	(Page 24)
Cue 4	**Sandy** switches on desk lamp *Snap on desk lamp and covering spot*	(Page 25)
Cue 5	**Baldo** switches on chandelier *Snap on chandelier, wall brackets and full interior lighting*	(Page 25)
Cue 6	**Alison** switches on table lamp *Snap on table lamp and covering spot*	(Page 25)
Cue 7	**Alison** switches on standard lamp *Snap on standard lamp and covering spot*	(Page 25)
Cue 8	**Baldo** switches off chandelier *Snap of chandelier, wall brackets and general interior lighting*	(Page 28)
Cue 9	**Baldo** switches off standard lamp *Snap off standard lamp and covering spot*	(Page 29)
Cue 10	**Baldo** switches off table lamp *Snap off table lamp and covering spot*	(Page 29)
Cue 11	**Sandy** switches on table lamp *Snap on table lamp and covering spot*	(Page 29)
Cue 12	**Sandy** switches off desk lamp *Snap off desk lamp and covering spot*	(Page 35)

ACT II, SCENE 1. Day

To open: General effect of warm early afternoon sunshine

Cue 13	**Sandy** exits *Fade to Black-out*	(Page 49)

ACT II, Scene 2. Day

To open: Darkness

Cue 14   As Scene opens   (Page 49)
            Fade up to late afternoon sunshine

Cue 15   **Sandy:** ". . . room for my father?"   (Page 59)
            Start slow fade to sunset and dusk

Cue 16   **Sandy, Alison** and **Baldo** switch on lights   (Page 60)
            Bring up general interior lighting

Cue 17   **Diana** stamps on the floor   (Page 65)
            Fountain lights up and plays

EFFECTS PLOT

ACT I

SCENE 1

Cue 1   AS CURTAIN rises   (Page 1)
Bells of Rome peal from outside windows: Italian tenor on radio

Cue 2   **Sandy** turns off radio   (Page 2)
Music off

Cue 3   **Wesley** enters   (Page 3)
Bells fade

Cue 4   **Baldo:** ". . . but it is not . . ."   (Page 8)
Telephone rings

Cue 5   **Baldo:** "We will not speak of money . . ."   (Page 9)
Telephone rings

SCENE 2

Cue 6   As Scene opens   (Page 24)
Telephone rings three times

Cue 7   **Trio** (*singing*): "Guide us to thy perfect . . ."   (Page 25)
Telephone rings

Cue 8   **Baldo:** "America!"   (Page 25)
Fade in Italian waltz on radio

Cue 9   **Baldo** switches off radio   (Page 26)
Bring music to full volume, then quickly off

Cue 10   **Alison:** "I didn't think you would."   (Page 31)
Bells of Rome peal

Cue 11   **Alison** studies wine label   (Page 32)
Bells fade a little

Cue 12   **Alison:** "It was super."   (Page 32)
Bells fade to silence

Cue 13   **Alison** and **Sandy** lean to kiss   (Page 35)
*Telephone rings, cuts off when **Sandy** jumps on floor*

ACT II

SCENE 1

Cue 14   **Alison** turns on radio   (Page 39)
Italian dance music

Cue 15   As **Alison** and **Sandy** dance   (Page 39)
Music cuts out

Cue 16   **Alison:** "Sandy!!"   (Page 47)
Telephone rings

SCENE 2

Cue 17	**Alison** turns on radio *Music—Italian tenor*	(Page 50)
Cue 18	**Sandy** turns off radio *Music off*	(Page 50)